July 2009 Consultation on the Professional Liaison Group's Recommendations to the Health Professions Council and the HPC's Standards of Proficiency for Counselling and Psychotherapy

# Compliance? Ambivalence? Rejection?

Nine papers challenging the Health Professions Council proposals for the State Regulation of the Psychological Therapies

**EDITED BY**
**DENIS POSTLE AND RICHARD HOUSE**

Linda Edwards MBACP
John Gloster-Smith MAHPP
Richard House IPN
Denis Postle IPN
Andy Rogers MBACP

Association for Group and Individual Psychotherapy
Arbours Association
Association of Independent Psychotherapists
Centre for Freudian Analysis and Research
The College of Psychoanalysts-UK
The Guild of Psychotherapists
Philadelphia Association
The Site for Contemporary Psychoanalysis

Foreword Professor Brian Thorne
Introduction Arthur Musgrave MBACP Accred., IPN
Afterword Professor Ian Parker

This Collection first published September 2009

A WLR/eIpnosis Production for the Alliance for Counselling and Psychotherapy Against State Regulation, supported by the Independent Practitioners Network

The Alliance for Counselling and Psychotherapy Against State Regulation
http://allianceforcandp.org/
info@allianceforcandp.org/

Independent Practitioners Network: http://i-p-n.org/
*e*Ipnosis: http://ipnosis.postle.net

Any surplus from sales of this book will be donated to the Alliance for Counselling and Psychotherapy Against State Regulation.



Our thanks to Arthur Musgrave and Steve Richards for essential production help.

**Compliance? Ambivalence? Rejection? Nine papers challenging the Health Professions Council July 2009 proposals for the State Regulation of the Psychological Therapies**

British Library Cataloguing in Publication Data
A catalogue record for this book is available from The British Library

ISBN 978-0-9545466-2-5

Wentworth Learning Resources [WLR] sailing barge 'Leonard Piper', The Mall, Chiswick, London W4 2PW wlr@postle.net

# Contents

**BRIAN THORNE** is Emeritus Professor of Counselling at the University of East Anglia, Norwich. He is an international figure in the world of person-centred psychotherapy and counselling.

# Foreword

Brian Thorne

It is with considerable reluctance that I find myself drawn back into the political fray by the issue of the statutory regulation of counsellors and psychotherapists. I retired from active practice as a therapist some three years ago after nearly forty years at the coal face, and much of the time these days I long for a reflective life where I can read, be quiet and cultivate my friendships. With Oscar Wilde I fondly imagine that I can now put my genius (such as it is) into my living rather than into my scribbling.

The current situation in the world of counselling and psychotherapy must sadly postpone such an idyllic prospect, for what follows in the pages of this passionate book shows all too clearly that the activity to which I have devoted the best part of my life is under threat. I have many colleagues for whom I have great respect who believe that by using such language I am over-reacting. They believe that statutory regulation is in any case inevitable and that the proposals currently before us may well do much to ensure professional credibility, improve standards and, above all else, enhance protection of some of the most vulnerable members of our society. I do not wish to question the integrity of those who hold that view, and I certainly have every sympathy with the resigned state of mind which believes the statutory regulation process to be inevitable. I have seen a similar stance, however, lead to helpless impotence in other professional arenas, most notably in the fields of education, health and social work. It is not perhaps irrelevant that it is precisely these areas of endeavour which attract those who are frequently inspired by an altruistic desire to be of service to their fellow human beings and who, sometimes against all the odds, continue to trust that humankind has within it the seeds of greatness.

It is the issue of trust which draws me back into the fray. In the pages that follow there are persuasive arguments which demonstrate – convincingly in my view – that the current proposals are ill-conceived, based on paltry evidence, threaten creativity in a field which has been notably creative and responsible, will diminish rather than extend sources of help for the vulnerable and, in any case, must fail to achieve the very objectives they are intended to accomplish. For me, however, all these valid arguments tend to pale into insignificance beside the high probability that if these proposals enter the statute book, they will constitute yet another powerful encouragement for individuals to be wary of their fellows and to assume that trustworthiness is in short supply and can only be uneasily 'guaranteed' by state certification. It is this erosion of trust – so manifestly demonstrated once again by the recent establishment of the new Independent Safeguarding Agency – that is fed by the hidden undercurrent running through these proposals. Sadly, the road to perdition is so often paved with good intentions, and in this instance the unwitting destructiveness comes wearing the cloak of hard-headed virtue and reasoned compassion for the vulnerable and the abused. It is powerfully seductive but so it has always been when the desire for power and control goes unrecognised by those who are seduced, and even sometimes by those who are convinced of their own benevolence. Lucifer, it should be remembered, was once the bearer of light.

**Brian Thorne,** Norwich, September 2009

**ARTHUR MUSGRAVE** lives and works in Bristol. He belongs to a Full Member Group of the Independent Practitioners Network and is accredited by BACP as a counsellor and supervisor.

# Introduction

Arthur Musgrave

In July 2009 the Health Professions Council [HPC] published a series of consultation questions alongside a report from its Professional Liaison Group [PLG], and draft standards of proficiency for the regulation of counselling and psychotherapy. The consultation period ends on 16th October 2009.

Here we publish a selection of material that will be submitted to the HPC. The first is a response by Andy Rogers to the consultation questions. It is followed by two critiques of the draft standards – one from a humanistic practitioner, John Gloster-Smith, and the other from Linda Edwards on behalf of the Adlerian Society of Wales. These need to be read in conjunction with the consultation documents: to download copies of these, see http://www.hpc uk.org/aboutus/consultations/index.asp?id=93 The next two pieces are by Denis Postle, who for more than a decade has hosted a website dedicated to scrutinising the dynamics of counselling and psychotherapy professionalisation: see http://ipnosis.postle.net/ These are followed by two more extended critiques. The first is a collective response from eight psychoanalytic bodies that is nonetheless searing in its criticisms. The second, by Richard House, is equally trenchant and sets this consultation in its wider context. Denis Postle concludes with the exploration of one of those trademark metaphors familiar to regular visitors to the eIpnosis website.

This collection is not an official Alliance response to the consultation, but instead reflects some of the diverse range of opinion within it. Yet there is surprising consensus. For as will be seen in what follows, practitioners from highly diverse vantage-points in the field have, quite independently, reached very similar conclusions on the HPC consultation documents – hence the existence of some repetition across the contributions that follow. It is quite clear that these HPC consultation documents could not have been drafted by anyone with an understanding of the field of counselling and psychotherapy. The standards of proficiency, for instance, mindlessly repeat generic standards that apply to other professions regulated by the HPC. Some of these are based on an inappropriate model of counselling and psychotherapy – 'the medical model' – that has been rejected following an exacting analysis of the published scientific research.[1] Others are obviously drafted with the needs of the NHS firmly in mind. In places the language is highly specific and irrelevant, while elsewhere it is hopelessly vague. Meaningful consultation cannot be undertaken in these circumstances.

The fundamental problem with HPC regulation is that none of the key principles "that should underpin statutory professional regulation" have been properly met. These were set out by the then Secretary of State for Health in 2007 in her introduction to the White Paper *Trust, Assurance and Safety.*[2] First, contrary to Patricia Hewitt's aspirations, issues of quality are clearly not paramount, nor are those of safety: the HPC has a slow, expensive and ineffective set of sanctions available that can allow those struck off to continue to practise – and this will continue to be the case, even if counselling and psychotherapy are eventually subjected to HPC regulation. Second, these recommendations do not have the confidence of the professionals involved – to date over 2,500 have signed a petition calling for a rethink and this total continues to grow. Third, while regulators are supposed to be independent of all interest groups involved in healthcare, the published standards of proficiency are blatantly skewed in favour of NHS management needs – and, it seems, the most blatantly inappropriate of these standards of proficiency, the generic ones, cannot be amended within the intended timescale of this legislative process. Fourth, statutory professional regulation, according to Patricia Hewitt, should be about "improving professional standards" - but there are powerful arguments in these papers that the opposite is the case. Fifth, professional regulation "should not create unnecessary burdens but should be proportionate to the risk it addresses". From the point of view of mainstream counsellors and psychotherapists, these recommendations create many burdens – see the list [in the letter to psychoanalytic colleagues] on page 65 – that would be laughable, if they were not such a serious imposition. Incidentally, how can anyone say what is "proportionate" without having something more than anecdotal evidence of risk on which to base a judgement? Finally, it is explicitly stated that HPC regulation needs to be "flexible" enough to address the needs of those operating outside the NHS. Such counsellors and psychotherapists represent the overwhelming majority of existing practitioners: even a cursory reading of the proposals out for consultation shows that their needs have not been addressed.

This failure to meet the criteria for success laid down at the outset ought in itself to be enough to send Government back to the drawing board. This legislative exercise has been deeply flawed from its inception. But the White Paper was confused in the task it set the HPC. On the one hand it predetermined the outcome by insisting that HPC regulation will happen – counsellors and psychotherapists "will be regulated by the Health Professions Council". On the other hand such regulation would only take place if the HPC were the right regulator – that is, HPC regulation would happen "following the HPC's rigorous process of" (a) "assessing their regulatory needs" and (b) "ensuing it is capable of accommodating them". But, if the HPC proved unsuitable, there was no alternative available ("the Government will not establish any new statutory regulators".) Bear in mind, too, that this was the first occasion on which Government initiated such a regulatory process – previously the HPC had waited for applications from aspirant groups. On top of this there has been no research to determine the nature and extent of the problem to which HPC regulation is supposed to be the remedy. To put it bluntly, this has been bad law making throughout.

These deficiencies now need to be confronted. The HPC should recommend to Government that it is not appropriate for it to proceed further. Government should then call a halt to HPC regulation and set up an enquiry that will (1) undertake research to identify the nature and scale of the problem to be addressed, (2) take account of all the relevant evidence, (3) build on best practice from around the world and (4) devise a scheme in which the benefits to the public exceed any negative unintended consequences.

---

[1] Wampold, Bruce E. (2001) *The Great Psychotherapy Debate: models, methods and findings.* London: Lawrence Erlbaum Associates

[2] Department of Health (2007) *Trust, Assurance and Safety.* London: HMSO

[3] ibid. para 7.16

**ANDY ROGERS** (MBACP) trained at the University of East Anglia and has since worked in student counselling for over ten years. He is a counsellor and counselling service coordinator for a large FE institution and a spare-time columnist for an independent therapy journal. He has written several papers on both the person-centred approach and the professional politics of therapy.

# Response to the HPC consultation on the potential statutory regulation of psychotherapists and counsellors

Andy Rogers, MBACP September 2009

*Please note: None of my responses below should be taken to suggest that a change in the proposals on a specific issue would make HPC regulation acceptable. I do not share the assumption of the consultation questions that the Register and the standards of proficiency should exist.*

**1. Do you agree that the Register should be structured to differentiate between psychotherapists and counsellors? If not, why not?**

The proposed differentiation between psychotherapists and counsellors is just one example (of many) demonstrating that regulation by the HPC is inappropriate and likely to have a negative overall impact on the field.

The specific error here is that at the level of actual practice – which presumably the Register and standards are principally concerned with – there are too many similarities between practitioners using different titles and, equally, too many *differences* between those using the *same* title, that it is impossible to meaningfully separate the titles themselves. Two 'psychotherapists' will quite feasibly have much *less* in common than might be found between a 'counsellor' and a 'psychotherapist' because issues of 'modality', practice context and the personal idiosyncrasies of the therapists in question will be far more significant in differentiating their work (and in accounting for differing client experiences) than their choice of title.

To treat the terms 'counsellor' and 'psychotherapist', then, as if they refer to distinct professional disciplines with clear demarcation is to ignore this central issue. The proposal, like many others in the draft, misunderstands the field and risks misinforming clients about the key choices in selecting a therapist.*

Furthermore, the proposed differentiation will legally sanction a hierarchy that currently exists only as a *disputed interpretation* of the structure of the profession. This present situation, where issues of professional identity can be debated and different viewpoints allowed to co-exist, is surely preferable to the proposal, which cements *in legislation* one view, one interpretation and one set of meanings, so that this one perspective becomes the pseudo-legitimate 'truth' even though many of us who use the titles in question would dispute its credibility. Here as elsewhere, the proposed regulation is at odds with the core values of the activity it seeks to regulate, against the wishes of a substantial portion of practitioners, an imposition rather than a 'working with' and, in the end, entirely unnecessary.

**2. Do you agree that the Register should not differentiate between different modalities? If not, why not?**

I do not accept the need for this type of register at all, but the proposal does reveal something else. By recommending not differentiating between 'modalities' – with their radically differing ethics, philosophies, values, practices, conceptions of the person and understandings of distress (such that many therapists would consider themselves to be doing something *fundamentally different* from those using other 'modalities') – and yet insisting on differentiating between counsellors and psychotherapists (where the apparent differences are complex, unclear and strongly contested), the proposals show themselves to be far removed from the realities of the profession, preferring a simplistic analysis suited to making regulation happen, rather than a genuine assessment of whether the form proposed is *suitable for* and *representative of* the field.

That said, neither would I wish to see an HPC Register that *does* differentiate between modality. The project of HPC regulation is founded on too many errors, misunderstandings and anti-therapeutic values to be redeemed by such a change.

**4. Do you agree that 'psychotherapist' should become a protected title? If not, why not?**

**5. Do you agree that 'counsellor' should become a protected title? If not, why not?**

No. I do not support either title becoming protected under the proposed system of regulation through the HPC. In many respects, to oppose the current draft proposals is the more 'values congruent' and therefore more *ethical* position for a large number of practitioners. Counselling and psychotherapy are not health professions, nor are they ancillary in most cases to medicine or healthcare. HPC is inappropriate – as briefly articulated in my other responses here – and the damage likely to be done to the field by this form of regulation far outweighs any possible benefit. *There is no substantive case nor evidence* to support the assertion that regulation of this type will sufficiently protect the public as claimed, while there are a number of full-length books that strongly suggest otherwise. (Postle D. *Regulating the Psychological Therapies: From Taxonomy to Taxidermy*, PCCS Books, Ross-on-Wye, 2007; Hogan D.B. *The Regulation of Psychotherapists***,** Ballinger, 1979; Mowbray R. *The Case Against* proposed regulation is at odds with the core values of the activity it seeks to regulate, against the wishes of a substantial portion of practitioners, an imposition rather than a 'working with' and, in the end, entirely unnecessary.

**2. Do you agree that the Register should not differentiate between different modalities? If not, why not?**

I do not accept the need for this type of register at all, but the proposal does reveal something else. By recommending not differentiating between 'modalities' – with their radically differing ethics, philosophies, values, practices, conceptions of the person and understandings of distress (such that many therapists would consider themselves to be doing something *fundamentally different* from those using other 'modalities') – and yet insisting on differentiating between counsellors and psychotherapists (where the apparent differences are complex, unclear and strongly contested), the proposals show themselves to be far removed from the realities of the profession, preferring a simplistic analysis suited to making regulation happen, rather than a genuine assessment of whether the form proposed is *suitable for* and *representative of* the field.

That said, neither would I wish to see an HPC Register that *does* differentiate between modality. The project of HPC regulation is founded on too many errors, misunderstandings and anti-therapeutic values to be redeemed by such a change.

**4. Do you agree that 'psychotherapist' should become a protected title? If not, why not?**

**5. Do you agree that 'counsellor' should become a protected title? If not, why not?**

No. I do not support either title becoming protected under the proposed system of regulation through the HPC. In many respects, to oppose the current draft proposals is the more 'values congruent' and therefore more *ethical* position for a large number of practitioners. Counselling and psychotherapy are not health professions, nor are they ancillary in most cases to medicine or healthcare. HPC is inappropriate – as briefly articulated in my other responses here – and the damage likely to be done to the field by this form of regulation far outweighs any possible benefit. *There is no substantive case nor evidence* to support the assertion that regulation of this type will sufficiently protect the public as claimed, while there are a number of full-length books that strongly suggest otherwise. (Postle D. *Regulating the Psychological Therapies: From Taxonomy to Taxidermy*, PCCS Books, Ross-on-Wye, 2007; Hogan D.B. *The Regulation of Psychotherapists*, Ballinger, 1979; Mowbray R. *The Case Against Psychotherapy Registration*, Trans Marginal Press, London, 1995; House R. & Totton N. (eds) *Implausible Professions: Arguments for Pluralism and*

*Autonomy in Psychotherapy and Counselling*, PCCS Books, Ross-on-Wye, 1997; Bates Y. & House R. (eds) *Ethically Challenged Professions*, PCCS Books, Ross-on-Wye, 2004; Parker I. & Revelli S. (eds) *Psychoanalytic Practice and State Regulation*, Karnac, London, 2008.)

On the specific issue of protecting 'counsellor', we should remember that the word 'counselling' was coined for the work by Carl Rogers (founder of the Person-Centred Approach and pioneer of humanistic psychology) precisely to facilitate a move away from the medicalised practices and professionalised bureaucracies of psychology and psychiatry. Rogers sought to humanise therapy both by reducing the power and status of the therapist as 'registered professional expert' and by demedicalising our understanding of distress – using the word 'counselling' was an essential part of that strategy.

To now appropriate the term, some half a century later, for a state registered 'health profession' that must conform to medicalised standards of proficiency is to attack the values that inspired this shift in the first place, and to steer counselling away from its client-centredness and back towards 'profession-centredness'.

So the HPC/PLG proposals are clearly not identifying what 'counselling' *is*, rather they are stating what they think it *should be*, replacing one cluster of meanings with another more rigid definition, which is opposed to the word's implied values in the professional context under consideration here. In so doing it changes fundamentally what it means to be a 'counsellor', despite the many thousands of practitioners who have trained and work using the term's original sense. Is this really within the remit of the HPC/PLG?

Further to these concerns, the unnecessary and fundamental shift that the proposed regulation entails – being redefined as a 'health profession' – has particular resonance in my own work as a counsellor in education, where many of us do not remotely consider ourselves to be health professionals, and the change threatens to radically alter our job descriptions, the values of our work and the way our students and staff perceive our services. It risks repositioning us to a degree that managers of our institutions could reasonably (but erroneously) consider us to be occupying the same practical territory (i.e. 'doing the same thing') as, say, an IAPT service.

Set the proposed regulation's redefining of counselling and psychotherapy in this broader professional context of NICE guidelines and the expanding IAPT scheme, which jointly discriminate against therapies with different research methodologies and evaluative philosophies (such as humanistic approaches which have a strong presence in student counselling), and enormous pressure could be exerted on college and university services to adopt evaluation procedures and therapeutic practices which are in conflict with their counsellors' core values – values proven to be uniquely suited to the character and demands of the educational setting.

Ultimately, as college and university management teams witness both the results of the steam-rollering of student counselling's unique character (homogeneity imposed upon a formerly diverse profession) and the parallel rise of community services that are highly problematic but nonetheless suited to the government's agenda and are superficially 'free' to the institution (e.g. IAPT), they could cut counselling services entirely. None of which would be a good thing for practitioners or the profession as a whole but, more importantly, *students* would lose out on having the *choice* of an accessible, embedded service with an invaluable depth of experience in the very context in which they find themselves.

**11. Do you think that the standards support the recommendation to differentiate between psychotherapists and counsellors?**

No. (Also see response to question 1.) The standards themselves are deeply flawed. Many psychotherapists *and* counsellors would take issue with both the medical model assumptions of the psychotherapist-specific standards ('disorder', 'treatment', 'symptoms') and the 'mental health' and 'wellbeing' model evident in the counsellor-specific standards.

In my own approach, the expression 'mental health' would not be considered sufficient for the subjects of counselling, which might be seen more usefully as existentially, relationally and/or socially derived, for example, rather than being considered matters of individual psychology (as 'mental health' implies). 'Well-being' is also not to be accepted uncritically, meaning as it does in most definitions, 'comfort', 'health' and 'happiness'. While these might be the prime concerns for some clients they are not for all, and counsellors would be naïve – if not unethical – to promise them as outcomes or even to promote them as states worth aspiring to. Each concept will in any case have a range of different meanings for different clients and different cultures.

With regard to the 'psychotherapist' standards, as a 'counsellor' it seems I would not (need to) be proficient in the 'diagnosis [and treatment] of severe mental disorders', but like many other therapists I would still tend towards a philosophical/political rejection of the underlying approach to human experience which these words and practices signify when they are attached to both distress and the professional responses that distress elicits or inspires. As Pete Sanders has written, a portion of person-centred therapists (psychotherapists and counsellors alike) advocate a 'principled and strategic opposition to the medicalisation of distress and all of its apparatus.' (Chapter in Joseph & Worsley, *Person-Centred Psychopathology*, PCCS Books, 2005)

**12. Do you think the standards are set at the threshold level for safe and effective practice? If not, why not?**

Notions of efficacy and safety are controversial in many approaches to counselling and psychotherapy. Some therapies reject the very idea that therapy should aim for 'effectiveness', which implies the instrumental application of techniques to achieve specific results. Instead, in this view, therapy is understood as a *principled space* for dialogue, encounter and exploration, a unique relationship with infinite possible 'outcomes', a *cultural* practice rather than a health-oriented one. (See Grant, B. The Imperative of Ethical Justification in Psychotherapy: The special case of client-centred therapy. *Person-Centred & Experiential Psychotherapies (PCEP). 2004; 3 (3): 152–165;* Howard, A. *Counselling and Identity – Self-Realisation in Therapy Culture.* Basingstoke: Palgrave Macmillan, 2005.)

On the question of safety, it is highly suspect to claim that any conversation or relationship can be 'safe' at all. It should also be noted that what might seem 'safe' to a regulator such as HPC – e.g. standards of proficiency and adversarial 'fitness to practise' hearings – might in fact be *damaging* to the authenticity of the person-to-person encounter in therapy and therefore potentially harmful to the client. The level of (oppressive) external authority imposed upon the relationship risks it being dominated by fear, or at least extreme caution, rather than the genuineness and openness to experience which might otherwise be aspired to. This in turn erodes the client's chances of, in person-centred language, 'internalising the locus of evaluation' – that is, trusting their own experiencing rather than deferring to external authority when making value judgements.

Most therapies have sufficient explanatory mechanisms to articulate how the professional and social environment can manifest in this way – as noxious influences in the psychological/relational experiences of the participants in therapy. That this has not been central to the work of the PLG is a disgrace.

**13. Are the draft standards applicable across modalities and applicable to work with different client groups?**

See my other responses with regard to the generally negative impact of such standards. In any case, we might well ask what 'client groups' are being referred to here? Some therapies, including person-centred therapy, do not see the categorisation or grouping of clients into types as particularly useful. Counsellors and psychotherapists of this kind prefer to see their clients (and therefore people generally) as unique and as having unique relationships with the socially or in some other way defined groupings or categories that might impact upon their experience.

**14. Do you think there are any standards which should be added, amended or removed?**

The whole standardisation process as proposed here is damaging to the practice of counselling and psychotherapy, therefore all the standards should be removed and the regulatory project in this particular form (HPC) abandoned. With others I call for a complete review of the entire regulation project to this point.

**15. Do you agree that the level of English language proficiency should be set at level 7.0 of the International English Language Testing System (IELTS) with no element below 6.5 or equivalent?** (Standard 1b.3)

> No (but nether do I think that changing this will make the standards as a whole acceptable). There are counsellors and psychotherapists who work mainly in a language other than English. I recently referred someone with little English themselves to a Polish counsellor, via an intermediary community organisation. The level of that counsellor's ability to speak English would have been irrelevant to their 'proficiency' with that client.

**16. Do you agree that the threshold educational level for entry to the Register for counsellors should be set at level 5 on the National Qualifications Framework? If not, why not?**

**17. Do you agree that the threshold educational level for entry to the Register for psychotherapists should be set at level 7 on the National Qualifications Framework? If not, why not?**

> My own counselling qualification is a *post-graduate diploma*, which is at the level required of those entering the proposed Register as a 'psychotherapist'. This highlights the error of differentiating counselling and psychotherapy on the basis of academic achievement. These thresholds also threaten to further restrict access to the professions for those experiencing social/economic disadvantage. Furthermore, there is *no evidence* that the educational level of the therapist correlates with the 'outcome' of therapy, nor with its 'safety' and 'efficacy' (even if we accept these terms uncritically). Why then should these levels be set at all? What purpose is served?

**18. Do you have any comments about the potential impact of the PLG's recommendations and the potential impact of statutory regulation?**

**19. Do you have any comments about the potential implications of this work on the future regulation of other groups delivering psychological therapies?**

**20. Do you have any further comments?**

See all previous responses.

Andy Rogers
September 2009

* As is common in the literature, I use the term 'therapist(s)' to refer to both 'counsellor(s)' and 'psychotherapist(s)'.

**JOHN GLOSTER-SMITH,** MAHPP, AC-accred., is a transpersonal group facilitator and coach working with personal and organisational clients and facilitating personal development programmes.

# Draft HPC Standards of Proficiency – a personal critique from a humanistic perspective

John Gloster-Smith, MAHPP

## Introduction

This brief commentary is a response to the Health Professions Council (HPC) Draft Standards of Proficiency which have been issued for consultation.

To get a clear flavour of what is likely to be the new regime for all psychotherapists and counsellors, the reader might profit by pausing at the very start of the Draft, and look at the "key". Here the authors state that the "HPC generic standards" are shown in black and that those specifically for psychotherapists and counsellors in blue and red. This distinction between the generic and the profession-specific is crucial. A quick glance may tempt the reader to think that the latter have been "slotted in" arbitrarily with the former. This is however no mere accident but a very clear and, for these professions, disastrous strategy by people who seem to be operating from administrative convenience and demonstrating that they do not understand the therapies they are claiming to be able to regulate. Thus no wonder there is a crisis of confidence within the professions with the HPC.

For this commentary therefore, it is useful to separate the psychotherapy and counselling standards from the generic standards.

## The generic HPC standards

These generic standards seem to be more suited to a health-care environment, for which I think they were prepared. The HPC is now bringing into this framework a very large group, perhaps the largest who probably in the main do not work in this mode. This is perhaps one reason why so many are having problems with it. These are very different professional worlds.

These health-care related issues have already been discussed elsewhere in Alliance for Counsellling and Psychotherapy Against State Regulation publications, but it might be useful just to list a few of the draft standards by way of reminder.

Registrant psychotherapists and counsellors, we are told, "must" demonstrate these standards. "Must" as a term will provoke uncomfortable reactions for humanistic practitioners, whose focus in their professional work is to support clients (not "patients") in liberating themselves from received social introjects. There is therefore immediately an incongruence between a seemingly parental if not paternalistic supervisory body, and the integrity of the therapist. It is therefore not surprising that the advent of the HPC is provoking such a crisis of conscience for practitioners, a contradiction between ownership of their professional world and externally imposed authority.

If we move on to look at some of the generic standards, here are some that the therapist "must" demonstrate. They "must", to quote

*be able to work, where appropriate, in partnership with other professionals, support staff, service users and their relatives and carers*

*understand the need to engage service users and carers in planning and evaluating diagnostics, treatments and interventions to meet their needs and goals*

*be able to contribute effectively to work undertaken as part of a multi-disciplinary team*

*be able to undertake and record a thorough, sensitive and detailed assessment, using appropriate techniques and equipment*

*be able to undertake or arrange investigations as appropriate*

*be able to use research, reasoning and problem solving skills to determine appropriate actions*

*be able to conduct appropriate diagnostic or monitoring procedures, treatment, therapy or other actions safely and skilfully*

*be able to gather information, including qualitative and quantitative data, that helps to evaluate the responses of service users to their care*

*be able to audit, reflect on and review practice*

*be aware of the role of audit and review in quality management, including quality control, quality assurance and the use of appropriate outcome measures*

*be able to maintain an effective audit trail and work towards continual improvement*

*participate in quality assurance programmes, where appropriate*

*understand the structure and function of the human body, relevant to their practice, together with knowledge of health, disease, disorder and dysfunction*

*be aware of the principles and applications of scientific enquiry, including the evaluation of treatment efficacy and the research process*

The therapist reader might be pardoned for their incredulity at this point, but these are the HPC's actual words. It should be very obvious to such a reader that many of these were written for a health-care group of professions. Yet this is a generic list of criteria. Psychotherapists and counsellors are not in the main health-care professionals. Thus for a psychotherapy or counselling practitioner, being compulsorily moved into the HPC orbit might seem like a highly artificial creation, one probably for administrative and public policy convenience. It is all the more likely that such practitioners will feel that this is not "their" body. This will probably heighten a defensive mentality when dealing with the body in question, rather than feel involved with a group committed to excellence in the profession for the benefit of all, both practitioners and ultimately and most importantly, the client.

## The psychotherapy and counselling draft standards

Reading the psychotherapy and counselling aspects separately however gives a different picture. From a humanistic perspective, there are clearly areas where they would have difficulties. However, one suspects this could partly be overcome by changes in wording that take more account of the differences. Yet, the more one reads through what has been produced, the more a humanistic practitioner may get an accumulating sense that what is being planned for her or his profession is something alien to their world.

These have been made clear in the comments in black against selected criteria, with the comments marked "J", for "John". The theoretical framework for illustrative purposes is Gestalt but this use of Gestalt terminology is not meant to be exclusive of other approaches within the humanistic field. The original wording in the draft standards is given in blue or red, with the draft's heading and item references also given to help find them in the text.

## Professional autonomy and accountability

### 1 a 1. Be able to practise within the legal and ethical boundaries of their profession

*Be able to recognise and manage the dynamics of power and authority*

J G-S: Setting aside the obvious preceding generic criteria in this section about boundaries and accountability, particularly to the "legal" framework, i.e. the HPC, a response from a humanistic perspective would be that to "recognise" and especially "to manage dynamics of power and authority" is a terminology that removes the client from being involved in developing awareness of their process and how they create relationships. It is also powerfully suggestive of the field conditions for the therapist now working within a context of externally imposed authority, which would be a contradiction of their orientation towards supporting the autonomy of the client.

## Professional relationships

### 1 b 1: be able to work, where appropriate, in partnership with other professionals, support staff, service users and their relatives and carers

*- be able to demonstrate sensitivity to organisational dynamics*

J G-S: It is highly likely that most therapists do not work within organisations and that this section as a whole is likely to be fairly meaningless to them. So to "demonstrate" such "sensitivity" would seem irrelevant, except as in being sensitive to the field conditions in which their client might live.

**1 b 4** *Be able to build, maintain and end therapeutic relationships with clients*

J G-S: Humanistically, we would describe the relationship as one that is co-created, not "built" by the therapist. Humanistically, we support clients in moving away from a world where things seem like they are "done to" them, and towards taking responsibility for what they create.

### Identification and assessment of health and social care needs

*- be able to devise a strategy and conduct and record the assessment process that is consistent with the theoretical approach, setting and client group*

*- be able to observe and record clients' responses and assess the implication for therapeutic work*

J G-S: Note that the generic heading is that of health care, not psychotherapy or counselling. With regard to the items in blue, the use of the word "assessment" might be one that is alien to many humanistic practitioners, although probably widely used by others in practice. It has connotations of remoteness from the client, a complete contrast from the warmth, aliveness and closeness of the relationship that so often occurs. It is also worth pointing out that many would not be recording "client's responses" in an actual session, since note-taking is often alien to the aliveness, contact and present-moment orientation of the work. "Client group" is a term a humanistic therapist might avoid, since it belongs with categorising people rather than affirming their uniqueness.

### Formulation and delivery of plans and strategies for meeting health and social care needs

J G-S: Once the managerial bits are taken out, almost all of this section is probably acceptable to humanistic practitioners. There is however one major objection. This major issue is the use of the term "**evidence-based practice**" in the generic framework in this section. While this might belong in the generic section just discussed, it is also referred to here because of its obvious therapeutic implication.

This term in my view is a Cognitive-Behavioural approach and actually one that belongs in one modality or group of modalities, and is emphatically NOT applicable across the range of psychotherapy and counselling professions as a whole. Here particularly the framework loses its impartiality, at a potential cost to certain widely-used modalities. Humanistic practitioners do not conceptualise their work in this manner. For example, a Gestaltist would rather be facilitating awareness in the client, by for example helping them become more aware of their own phenomenology, and the practitioner would regard that as within their own field of awareness, which is likely to be different to that of the therapist. The "evidence" would then become the client's own evidence, one to be explored together with the therapist. To speak of "evidence", as the generic standards do, would then simply be an invitation to a humanistic practitioner to share a perception and therefore only a partial and subjective perspective on what is occurring in the work. Such pseudo-scientific jargon is meaningless in this context.

Use of "evidence" jargon will heighten the sense in the practitioner of being hijacked by a specific modality, which is already occurring elsewhere, for example in the way the NHS has been switching to CBT, and which is not actually proven to have the pre-eminence that its proponents claim.

2 b 4 *Be able to establish an effective, collaborative working relationship with the client*

> *- be able to initiate and manage first and subsequent counselling / psychotherapy sessions by developing rapport and trust*

J G-S: The words "to establish", "initiate and manage" and "developing rapport and trust" are problematical for humanistic practitioners, as they suggest something "being done" by the therapist. As stated above they would see the process as co-created and would seek to support the client in taking responsibility and creating rapport. They may for example have very poor rapport "skills" and have an issue with trusting people. The very work might be about learning to trust the therapist and then to extend that to their relationships. Humanistically, we might say that we become able to trust and do not have our trust "developed" by someone else. It is an internal not an external process. The words used here, however, seem to come right out of an NHS manager's competency framework.

## Critical evaluation of the impact of, or response to, the registrant's actions

## Knowledge, understanding and skills

**3 a 1. Know and understand the key concepts of the bodies of knowledge which are relevant to their profession-specific practice**

J G-S: Despite the reference to psychopathology in the text, there are well-established ways of looking at this topic that humanistic practitioners can work with that are not necessarily or only from the *DSM IV*. The latter is more associated with the clinical psychology world. In Gestalt this might be explored, for example, through a client's "style of relating in the world" or his or her "Interruptions to Contact". However, the use of the term "psychopathology" can be problematic to certain humanistic practitioners, with its mental health associations.

Now, to take some of the sub-sections listed in the draft Standards:

*"mental and emotional health", "mental disorder", "common / general mental health problems".*

J G-S: Humanistic practitioners do not tend to regard what a client is experiencing as within a "health/illness" polarity. This sharply distinguishes them from a mental health/psychiatric perspective. "Order/disorder" is not a humanistic way of conceptualising a person's process. To my example from Gestalt, this modality would see her or his "process" as a "creative adjustment" and would be wary of categorising people.

The standards in this section then move to a very controversial area, where psychotherapists and counsellors are treated differently.

J G-S: In the sub-sections for psychotherapists separate from counsellors, and visa versa, highly controversial distinctions seem to be made that suggest that psychotherapists deal with more severe levels of disorder than counsellors. This ignores the work that has been done over the last few decades that has led to the view that the two professions cannot be so clearly distinguished. The HPC would appear to be on very shaky ground here.

Psychotherapists for example "must" exclusively be able to

- *conduct appropriate diagnostic procedures*
- *understand and implement treatment methods to address symptoms and causes of severe mental disorder*

J G-S: Humanistic practitioners would have particular issues here, since the terms "diagnostic procedures", "treatment" and "symptoms" would to many of them, I suspect, smack of a "mental health" and *DSMIV* model of responding to human pain, more appropriate to an NHS environment and psychiatry. Diagnosis would remove the client from involvement in working on themselves and make them more of a patient for whom a set of treatments would be devised, as in the health-care model.

## Conclusion

To me, the fundamental weaknesses of these draft proficiencies are the apparent attempt to put them into a health-care context, a tendency towards a behavioural bias in terms of the over-arching theoretical model used, and a health-care managerial mind-set in terms of practical application. It is not surprising therefore that so very many practitioners, who in the main do not see themselves as health practitioners, feel that this project is "not for them". Moreover these draft standards emphasise how misconceived is the whole project of the Health Professions Council regulation of psychotherapy and counselling.

John Gloster-Smith, MAHPP
Calne, Wiltshire
August 2009.

**LINDA EDWARDS** is an Adlerian psychotherapist and trainer based in Narberth, Pembrokeshire for the last eleven years. Before then she lectured in Education at King's College, London where she directed PGCE and MA research and authored books on philosophy and world religions. Her focus now is on making the psychology of Alfred Adler available and better known in West Wales.

# Response to the HPC Draft Standards of Proficiency for Psychotherapists and Counsellors from the Adlerian Society of Wales

Linda Edwards MBACP

There are a number of issues of concern which recur repeatedly throughout this document. These will be listed as a summary before proceeding to comment about the Draft Standards of Proficiency.

1) The language and structure of the HPC is focussed on the medical world – references to the use of equipment, to infection control, and to the wearing of protective clothing. This leads us to ask the question of how much knowledge and understanding the Council has acquired during the last three years or so when it has been in discussion. Most of what is written clearly does not apply to counselling and psychotherapy.

2) The view of therapy assumed by the HPC is seen as a procedure applied to a passive patient. This is evidenced by the language of the document which consistently describes a patient as passive in receiving help from a team of experts in their field. This view is not only at odds with Adlerian psychotherapy which involves a relationship between two equals (one of which is skilled in therapy), but also contradicts the main work of Humanistic therapy per se, which is carried out not by the therapist but by the patient. Hence the patient is the active agent in the whole process starting from the very first phone call they make to get help. And dynamic relations between patient and therapist are the central component of the work.

3) The draft standards rely on procedures such as audit, management and predetermined outcome which are the antithesis of counselling and psychotherapy. If applied in the way suggested by the HPC, the private space afforded by therapy would become more like an examination room. The consequences of this on therapeutic practice would be destructive. The irony is clear in some schools of Adlerian and Humanistic psychotherapy, where we define the counselling process as the effort to free oneself from the internalised critical judge that may be the initial cause of the patient's unhappiness.

4) Finally, the Standards rely on a view of the self which is discarded by Adlerian psychologists world-wide. The assumptions behind the HPC include seeing human beings as faulty, somehow needing repair, and

then needing to be continually upgraded. Whereas in reality human beings are very creative, and from infancy create beliefs about self, others and the world which influence their childhood behaviour and eventually lead them to habitually act and behave the way they do in adult life. When someone presents the Adlerian therapist with bi-polar disorder or OCD they are not viewed as "ill" or "mentally dys-functional" as though they had a symptom to be removed. They are viewed as creative individuals who have (mostly) unconsciously put problematic behaviour in place to make sure life does not get worse. This means we ask, "What is the purpose of this behaviour?", not what is wrong with this person, or what condition does this person have. Not a psychology of "possession" but a psychology of "use".

## Commentary on the Draft Standards

**NB**: Although we occasionally use the term 'patient' rather than 'client' which is the term used in counselling, we do not intend to convey a passive or medicalised position, but rather that of an active person in the therapeutic process.

We have not addressed every point but have prioritised those that most concern us.

**Point 1A.1** The point that psychotherapists and counsellors must '*understand the need to respect, and so far as possible uphold, the rights, dignity, values and autonomy of every service user including their role in the diagnostic and therapeutic process and in maintaining health and wellbeing*'.

We do not see ourselves as doctors or health professionals. Counselling and therapy provide a respectful space for a conversation with and about the patient, rather than delivery of healthcare. Similarly, we would see it on occasion, as a central part of our work, to respectfully confront the value systems of the patient. The clash of values can be a crucial instrument of change within therapeutic practice.

**1A.6** The requirement that psychotherapists and counsellors must be able *'to assess a situation, determine the nature and severity of the problem and call upon the required knowledge and experience to deal with the problem'* is not acceptable. This is a medicalised view of psychotherapy where there is a problem to be defined and a procedure put in place to deal with it. The care of the patient may or may not include problem solving. For example the devoted 84 year old whose partner dies cannot solve "the problem" – the "cure" is in the process and the long-term tasks of mourning and grief.

The danger here is that the HPC approach of problem-solving and solution focussed work are used as definitive of good standards and then used to either exclude or sanction alternative therapeutic approaches. Adlerian psychotherapists do not see their job as solving problems.

**1A.8** The requirement that psychotherapists and counsellors '*understand both the need to keep skills and knowledge up to date and the importance of career long learning*' needs to be unpacked and understood in relation to psychotherapy. The kind of knowledge operative in psychotherapy is often unconscious knowledge rather than academic knowledge which is easy in transmission. Training in psychotherapy involves profound inner psychological awareness and change, and it is this change that will allow the person to work with other people as a therapist without confusion or neglect of important psychological boundaries. The focus here is on personal development in order to open oneself up to another human being. The fact that this perspective is central to a large number of established traditions of psychotherapy, and a requirement on diploma training courses, must be recognised in any consideration of proposed standards of proficiency.

The requirement that psychotherapists and counsellors must be able to recognise '*their own distress and disturbance and be able to develop self care strategies*': Self- Knowledge and Self Awareness are at the heart of the our approach. However, the danger with this requirement as stated is that the therapist is seen as a kind of manager whose job involves risk management of the patient whilst managing and auditing the self. Perhaps there are some practitioners who hold this view but Adlerians do not.

**1B.1** The requirement that psychotherapists and counsellors '*understand the need to build and sustain professional relationships as both an independent practitioner and collaboratively as a member of a team*' may apply to those working in the NHS but will not apply to many of us who work in private practice and who are clear about the importance of independence. Some patients will prefer this setting rather than a group or corporate setting. This does not discount the need for professional accountability, but rather respects the value of independence and choice for both the therapist and for the client.

The requirement that psychotherapists and counsellors '*understand the need to engage service users and carers in planning and evaluating the diagnostics, treatment and interventions to meet their needs and goals*' might be important to those therapies which focus on targeted interventions, but is not relevant to therapies which offer an open exploration of human life situations. Epistemologically, the HPC and Adlerian Psychology are at odds here. Evaluating diagnostics, treatments and interventions is a medical paradigm that *puts the patient in the position of an object, to whom a treatment is applied*, i.e. in the "one up" (practitioner) and "one down" patient position. The ethos in our form of counselling is for negotiation where the client and the counsellor work together to form an hypothesis upon which therapy can take place. This hypothesis is then tested by the client as to how it resonates and fits with them. This puts the patient on an equal footing with the therapist. Any notion of inferiority or being "less than" is never acceptable.

Furthermore, Adlerian psychotherapy often aims specifically not to meet the needs and goals of the patient – to do so would tie in with their *Private Logic,* i.e. their beliefs about self, others and the world which underpin their socially useless behaviour. Any therapy which recognises that needs and goals may be unconscious phenomena, formulated in the conscious world as demands and behaviour, means that the therapist has an ethical obligation to listen to the client at an unconscious level. This is central in all psychoanalytic therapies, where the idea of meeting the patient's needs and goals would be unthinkable. In fact, therapy would mean the refusal of the analyst to meet the patient's demand.

**1B.2** The requirement that psychotherapists and counsellors *'be able to contribute effectively to work undertaken as part of a multidisciplinary team'* may be applicable to certain therapists working in the NHS but has no application to those of us in private practice therapy or counselling.

**1B.3** The requirement that psychotherapists and counsellors must *'be able to demonstrate effective and appropriate skills in communicating information, advice, instruction and professional opinion to colleagues, service users, their relative and carers'* may be applicable to health professionals, but the confidentiality of client material, not advice or instruction to *"colleagues ... relatives and carers"*, is paramount in Adlerian Counselling.

The next requirement, that *therapists and counsellors be able to communicate in English to Level 7 of the international English language testing system* does not sit easily with psychotherapy. This is because language itself could form part of the transference process a client needs in order to do the personal work on themselves. For example, if a client had a mother who was unable to speak clearly the language of the country in which they lived, they may unconsciously identify with a therapist who does not have "appropriate *communication skills"*. To require proficiency in the English language undermines the client's freedom of choice and their opportunity to work on their relationship with their mother via the therapist.

The requirement that psychotherapists and counsellors be *'able to communicate appropriately and effectively with other professionals about the client and propose therapeutic work'* reiterates what can be found all through the HPC document, that a patient is someone about whom other professionals may discuss. This shows just how central to the HPC draft is the medical model where professional others discuss a patient as the recipient of interventions done to them. In contrast, for Adlerians, the patient is an active person and the main work of therapy is undertaken not by the therapist but by the patient.

**1B.4** The requirement that psychotherapists and counsellors *'understand the need for effective communication throughout the care of the service user'* needs clarification. For example – what notion of communication are we talking about and what theory of efficacy is assumed? If a therapist was silent for a whole session – this might be seen as effective communication by one client but as non communication by another. Silence can be a space in which the patient can hear themselves in a new way. Some therapists would see the idea of communicating information to the client as non-professional in that it can be seen as the therapist making suggestions to the client which then places the therapist in a superior role as expert, a situation which Adlerians would wish to avoid.

The requirement that psychotherapists and counsellors '*be able to build, maintain and end therapeutic relationships with clients'* seems rather straightforward but it again points to something applied to the patient, rather than seeing therapy as the work done by the patient. It is really the work of the client to build, maintain and end the therapeutic relationship, albeit the therapist facilitates this to the best of their ability. This practice of negotiation is something that is consistently unrepresented in HPC's standards of proficiency.

**2A.2** The requirement that psychotherapists and counsellors '*be able to select and use appropriate assessment techniques*' may apply to some therapists who work diagnostically, but we aim to avoid objectifying a patient through 'assessing' them. This also applies to the following requirement, *that psychotherapists and counsellors 'be able to undertake and record a thorough, sensitive and detailed assessment, using appropriate techniques and equipment'*.

The following requirement obliges psychotherapists and counsellors to '*be able to devise a strategy and conduct and record the assessment process that is consistent with the theoretical approach, setting and client group'*. We do not accept, *a priori*, that there is such a thing as a 'client group': we work with each unique individual who presents themselves. The objection to making client groups out of individuals is that it imposes classification structures rather attending to the uniqueness of each individual.

The section entitled '*Formulation and delivery of plans and strategies for meeting health and social care needs*': We would not necessarily recognise that as counsellors we are there to meet the health and social care needs of their patients. Often what we have to offer in the counselling room is a process which contrasts with the health and social care model of care.

**2B.1** The requirement that psychotherapists and counsellors *'be able to use research, reasoning and problem solving skills to determine appropriate action'* may be appropriate at times in Adlerian therapy, as it is here that we co-incide with other cognitive-based therapies. However, the next requirement that psychotherapists and counsellors *'be able to engage in evidence based practice, evaluate practice systematically, and participate in audit procedures'* is symptomic of a growing therapeutic culture which is flawed in its very premises. "Evidence-based research" is marketed as 'best practice' for different particular symptoms, and when accepted as "truth" drives the funding process, thus financing no-cost counselling (e.g. IAPT) which in turn affects experienced therapists in the field in that their client base diminishes. As choice of counsellors diminishes, so does patient choice. The Adlerian Society of Wales would not accept the notion of audit procedures which is linked to the world of business or managed health care rather than to the individual and creative work that is the process of psychotherapy.

The following requirement that psychotherapists and counsellors *'be able to demonstrate a level of skill in the use of information technology appropriate to their practice'* has nothing to do with psychotherapy and counselling. The recording of client information on computers is highly controversial as confidentiality can often not be ensured. A client above all needs to feel emotionally and psychologically safe with the counsellor to enable therapeutic discussion and interventions of change which are often difficult and challenging to emerge.

The requirement that psychotherapists and counsellors *'be able to make informed judgements on complex issues in the absence of complete information'* is clearly misplaced in the draft document. Here is the medical model again, where information may be necessary about health issues prior to the prescription of medication or surgery. Even to assume that complete information is tenable is a fallacy.

**2B.3** The requirement that psychotherapists and counsellors *'be able to formulate specific and appropriate management plans including the setting of timescales'* will probably suit counsellors working in NHS settings where funding is released for time-limited work, but this has little to do with the open-ended work of psychotherapy where often counsellor and client contract together for as long as the work might take, and where both parties negotiate that time together. In fact the very idea of a 'management plan' is nigh on impossible because of the fallacy of trying to predict in advance what will happen in the therapy. More and more as the HPC document is read and assimilated, it feels like a neurosis of mega-control trying to destroy what is a creative, holistic and benevolent profession which is already regulated by reputable professional organisations like BACP who understand the conceptual and experiential world in which therapists work.

**2B.4** The requirement that psychotherapists and counsellors *'be able to conduct appropriate diagnostic or monitoring procedures, treatments, therapy or other actions carefully and skilfully'*: As we have already mentioned, different forms of therapy would not accept the notion of diagnostic or 'monitoring procedures'.

The requirement that psychotherapists and counsellors '*understand the need to maintain the safety of both service users and those involved in their care'* needs explanation. What notion of safety is this? Ethical psychotherapists would wish to work in an environment which is safety conscious, but the maintaining of safety in terms of health is the responsibility of the patient, not the duty of the therapist.

On a more subtle level, there is a danger of therapists colluding with the fantasy (conscious or unconscious) that it is possible to attempt to control the therapeutic process, and render it safe. The paradox is that the illusion of safety can end up being *more* dangerous for clients than the status quo. For example, those institutions which surround themselves with "Mission Statements" may discover they are examples of false illusion – the wording is therapeutic, but the neglect and ineffectual treatment given to patients can be masked by words, and codes of behaviour have a different and often hidden tale to tell.

The requirement that psychotherapists and counsellors *'be able to establish an effective, collaborative working relationship with a client'*: Psychotherapy is not something that the counsellor gives to the client, but is rather a dynamic relationship between two people. It is unacceptable to require the psychotherapist to establish an effective collaborative relationship because the relationship will also be the responsibility of the client.

The requirement that psychotherapists and counsellors '*be able to enable and work with expression of client emotion'* is not acceptable because there are very different schools of thought about the role and function of emotion in the counselling process. Some schools of psychotherapy see no great value on the expression of emotion, rather what matters are the unconscious thought processes within. On this view, emotions may be misleading. Other therapies emphasise the expression and release of emotion as part of the therapy but there is no agreed view.

The requirement that psychotherapists and counsellors '*be able to communicate empathic understanding to clients'*: Whereas Adlerian therapists would agree with this statement, it would not be accepted by other schools of psychotherapy who believe there should be emotional distance between therapist and client. This means that listening could well be attentive but not empathic, for empathy implies that the internal states of the patient are accessible and can be wholly or partly shared by the therapist. There is no consensus on this issue.

The requirement that psychotherapists and counsellors '*be able to respect and take into account the client's capacity for self determination*' does not hold if self-determination is to have no self-determination. This is what so often happens to long-term cannabis (skunk) users who are patients. Their self-determination is to have no motivation for anything socially useful and they feel trapped in their own self-determination. The issue of self-determination gets even more complex when, for some schools of therapy, autonomy and self-determination are fictions.

The requirement that psychotherapists and counsellors '*be able to work with both the explicit and implicit aspects of the therapeutic relationship*' is difficult to understand.

**2B.5** The requirement that psychotherapists and counsellors '*be able to keep accurate, legible records and recognise the need to handle these records and all other information with applicable legislation, protocol and guidelines*' is not problematic to most Adlerians who record the Early Memories of the client and details of family constellation etc., and keep them carefully confidential. But many psychoanalysts are against record keeping because they believe it blocks the spontaneity of unconscious communication between patient and analyst.

The requirement that psychotherapists and counsellors '*understand the need to use only accepted terminology in making records*' is either madness or badness and we are not sure which.

A) If it is madness it implies that there is such a thing as accepted terminology in psychotherapy. What would terminology include? "collective unconscious?", super-ego?", "gemeinschaftesgefuhl", "biased apperception?".

B) If it is badness then therapists, in using acceptable terminology, will allow themselves to be shaped and moulded and eventually influenced to think about their work through the eyes of some unseen bureaucrat – either a benevolent bureaucrat or a psychotic dictator. When this happens, and the minds and practice of psychotherapist are influenced by a third party, then the practice of psychotherapy is dead, and freedom of thought and practice is dead.

**2C.1** The requirement that psychotherapists and counsellors '*be able to monitor and review the ongoing effectiveness of planned activity and modify it accordingly*' is not acceptable in therapies where the counsellor does not plan activity. Where therapy seeks to address the needs of the client in the here and now, where it recognises that there are ongoing unfolding conversations of depth where interventions may or may seem appropriate, then applying specific procedures of monitoring and checking are seen as relevant only when summary or synopsis would help the client, not as a requirement.

The requirement that psychotherapists and counsellors *'be able to evaluate intervention plans using recognised outcome measures and revise the plans as necessary in conjunction with the service user'*:This kind of language comes directly from the NHS and has little or no application to Adlerian psychotherapy. Our world does not involve intervention plans that are then applied to the patient as the recipient of a procedure, and there is no notion of 'recognised outcome measures'. In psychotherapy, the psychotherapist listens to what the client has to say.

The requirement that psychotherapists and counsellors *'recognise the need to monitor and evaluate the quality of practice and the value of contributing to the generation of data for quality assurance and improvement programmes'* is acceptable if by that it means that clients can anonymously (to avoid lack of objectivity) give feedback to the counsellor or therapist and that feedback then informs future practice. But if it implies the task of a therapist managing the patient, then the task undermines the mutual process of therapy and the sense of equality of client and counsellor in the process. In addition,'quality assurance' is unacceptable to schools of psychotherapy that are not based on a business model of service provision.

The requirement that psychotherapists and counsellors *'be able to make reasoned decisions to initiate, continue, modify or cease treatment for the use of techniques or procedures, and record the decision and reasoning appropriately'* raises the question of why every clinical decision would need to be recorded and explained. This means taking on board an approach to counselling in which what the therapist does would only be valid given a designated other person affirming their practice. This feels more like a police state, and is about as far from the ethos of psychotherapy as you can get. Good supervisors often ask counsellors about techniques and procedures and their efficacy, sometimes suggesting further methods or monitoring the rationale for their usage. The proposed requirement is already partly adhered to in a formative and normative way in the supervision process.

**2C.2** T The requirement that psychotherapists and counsellors *'understand the principles of quality control and quality assurance'* is problematic in that it is the language of the consumer-led market place. At the heart of Adlerian psychotherapy is to provide a space outside our consumer-led culture. In this space human beings are not seen as 'resources'. We would never use business vocabulary to describe the process we undertake with clients.

The requirement that psychotherapists and counsellors *'be able to maintain an effective audit trail and work towards continued improvement'*: This business language is getting worse – now we have metaphors of accountancy and audit. Adlerians do not even believe in the idea of 'continual improvement'. So much therapy for human suffering and dysfunction is all about integrating or accepting or reframing experiences of trauma, loss or fragmentation at the heart of human experience. In contrast it is the “well-being” industry which focuses on ‘continual improvement’, so that they can sell more and more products to people. We do not sell therapy or make promises to the public about results.

**3A.1** The requirement that psychotherapists and counsellors ‘*understand the structure and function of the human body, relevant to their practice, together with knowledge of health, disease, disorder and dysfunction*’: Adlerian therapists, like Alfred Adler (1870-1937) their mentor, focus on the body, but not in the way assumed by mainstream medicine. We adhere to the belief of Holism, that is, the indivisible connection between mind and body. To see a physical condition is also to see a mental condition and vice versa.

The requirement that psychotherapists and counsellors ‘*be aware of the principles and application of scientific enquiry, including the evaluation of treatment efficacy and the research process*’ is not unreasonable to us, but not if that means a biased conception of scientific enquiry, efficacy and research, for example, scientific enquiry *á la* primary model of CBT which is then used as a protocol to evaluate therapeutic practice.

The requirement that psychotherapists and counsellors ‘*understand the typical presentations of severe mental disorder*’: We are critical of how psychiatric models of mental disorder are used as a benchmark in the evaluation of therapeutic practices.

Adlerian Psychology generally acquaints its students and practitioners with the DSM IV not as a diagnostic measure but as an important tool in recognising different behaviours as an aid to observation, and to enable appropriate conversation with both clients and the medical profession. For us, a client uses behaviour, even ‘mentally disordered behaviour’, either to avoid feeling grossly inferior or to elevate themselves to perceived superiority as in the grandiose behaviours. Thus the client is a creator of their universe, not a victim of a condition or disease.

**3A.2** The requirement that psychotherapists and counsellors *‘select or modify approaches to meet the needs of an individual, group or community’* might apply to some, but not for example to psychoanalysts, where it is only ethical if the analyst is skilled in refusal to meet the needs of the patient.

**3A.3** The requirement that psychotherapists and counsellors ‘*be aware of applicable health and safety legislation and any relevant safety policies and procedures in force in the workplace, such as incident reporting, and be able to act in accordance with these*’ is obviously valid if you are working in NHS contexts, less so in private practice. Of course, having said this, there are basic measures taken to ensure that the consulting room does not contain unsafe conditions.

The requirement regarding '*hazard control and particularly infection control*': It is startling that such a requirement has been applied to this draft document on counselling and psychotherapy, especially since the HPC has taken some three years to think about it.

**Adlerian Society of Wales** August 2009

**DENIS POSTLE** is a writer, artist and musician who has been a facilitator of personal and professional development since 1985. A founder participant in the Independent Practitioners Network [IPN] he sees that organisation as demonstrating that long term civic accountability for clients and psychopractitioners can be structured through cooperative, non hierarchical organisations.

The Health Professions Council Draft Standards of proficiency for psychotherapy and counselling, July 2009

# Scorpio*n* Rising

Denis Postle

> *An encounter with a black scorpion is not likely to be problematic; you probably see it before it sees you. It's the transparent ones that are almost invisible which are dangerous and the most poisonous.*
>
> *Household hint, France*

If, as seems to be the case with many practitioners, you are sitting with considerable ambivalence about the value of State Regulation for clients, for yourself and for the field, what might you need to know?

As I have long argued, there is an over-arching aspect of the HPC's actions that merits your attention and which should be kept in mind in reading what follows. As an instrument of the state, the HPC's values, especially their power relations, are of the 'power over' variety; 'power with' consultations and the PLG meetings have consistently proved to be public relations exercises concerned with ticking the regulator's performance criteria boxes.

HPC personnel are amiable, transparent and accessible, their processes exude modernity and reasonableness. However this is a culture of domination, and everything that the Professional Liaison Group [PLG] has recommended in the draft standards of proficiency that we will look at here has been produced via a process of collaboration under duress, and which can be expected to be enforced by the HPC with matching duress.

Why does this matter? Because as a practitioner I'd be surprised if you didn't follow a way of working with clients that was as far as possible free of duress, and that you'd be aware that the abuse that many clients show up with is in one way and another the result of 'power over' bullying, excessive or unjustified force, manipulation, victimisation or discrimination, i.e. duress. Exactly the qualities that the HPC as a regulator brings to its capture of the psychological therapies. How can such a culture of coercion as the HPC embodies fail eventually to contaminate, restrict or skew the work you do?

Does this seem far-fetched? Let's look first at how your professional representatives have decided that as a practitioner you will be expected to behave. The 'Standards of proficiency for psychotherapists and counsellors' document is an 11pp catalogue of injunctions: it lists 68 items that begin with 'be able to', 40 that begin with 'understand', 5 that begin with 'recognise', and 3 with 'be aware of'. Not that controversial you might think, until you look at how the document frames these items (more on that anon).

On page 2 is a headline that applies to everything that follows – Registrant psychotherapists and counsellors **must:**

This word 'must' is the key to the whole document. By joining the HPC register you take on a legal obligation to adhere to these 'abilities', 'understandings', 'recognitions' and 'awarenesses'. And if it still isn't clear, you buy into a system of coercion and duress that has at its end point legally binding 'fitness to practice' hearings based on these standards that are sharply adversarial in style.

Keeping this over-arching culture of coercion in mind, let us look into the 'consultation draft' of the 'Standards of proficiency for psychotherapists and counsellors'. **I'll add in italics the missing element of duress:** *you must.* In the original document, text in blue applies to psychotherapists and counsellors, and red where it is only applicable to either counsellors or psychotherapists; alongside this I have tried to keep the original formatting.

> **1a.1** – *you must* understand the need to respect, and so far as possible uphold, the rights, dignity, values and autonomy of every service user including their role in the diagnostic and therapeutic process and in maintaining health and wellbeing

Do you have a 'diagnostic process'? Can you willingly or ethically undertake to 'uphold the values' of every service user?

> *- you must be able to recognise and manage the dynamics of power and authority*

Yes… and might this also include being able to recognise and reject (or at least discuss) inappropriate regimes of power and authority such as that entailed by HPC regulation?

> **1a.2** - *you must* **be able to practise in a non-discriminatory manner**

Yes, laudable. The HPC requires it but has consistently demonstrated discrimination against other ways of generating civic accountability in favour of its pre-existing approach to regulation. See my account of the first PLG meeting[1] for how this has been done.

> **1a.4** - *you must* **understand the importance of and be able to obtain informed consent**

Informed consent for what? This seems another indicator of a 'power over' coercive culture in which something is to be done *to* a client for which informed consent must be obtained. See later the use of the word 'apply'.

> **1a.6** - *you must* **be able to practise as an autonomous professional, exercising their own professional judgement**
>
> *you must* be able to assess a situation, determine the nature and severity of the problem and call upon the required knowledge and experience to deal with the problem.

"Assess a situation?" Many practitioners would see themselves as exploring perceptions of a "situation" (including the naming of it as a "situation"). And then "problem" is a potentially narrow perception of experience: it may be that the extent to which a client sees something as a problem might often interfere with *their* ability to develop resources to "deal" with "it".

> - *you must* be able to initiate resolution of problems and be able to exercise personal initiative

Again this presumes a practitioner 'managing'/'controlling' the relationship with the client.

> - *you must* know the limits of [your] practice and when to seek advice or refer to another professional
>
> - *you must* recognise that [you] are personally responsible for and must be able to justify [your] decisions.

Why is it necessary to include this? As soon as the injunction 'you must' is added there is something about these lines that more than hints at a parent talking to an errant teenager.

This suggests that we might usefully look at the potential 'fitness to practice' version – if for 'able to' we substitute 'failure':

> - *you failed* to assess the situation, determine the nature and severity of the problem and call upon the required knowledge and experience to deal with the problem
>
> - *you failed* to initiate resolution of the problems and were unable to exercise personal initiative

Very subtle nuances of the therapeutic alliance are freeze-dried into 'nature and severity', making it an object to which knowhow can be applied, as though definition of 'being able to' somehow disposed of what 'failed to' might entail in a fitness to practise hearing.

Lets hold this reversal for a moment and use it to look at 1a.7 and 1a.8, which screw down the generic HPC notion of 'fitness to practise' that as a registrant you would be legally contracted to deliver.

> **1a.7 - *you failed to* recognise the need for effective self-management of workload and resources and be able to practise accordingly**

This seems to imply that if on occasion you put yourself out in exceptional ways that other practitioners saw as interfering with their status or employment prospects, this could count as a failure of self-management. These standards already appear to have provided a rich field for denunciations based on interpersonal rivalries in other regulated professions.

> **1a.8** - *you failed to* **understand the obligation to maintain fitness to practise**
>
> - *you failed* to understand the need to practise safely and effectively within your scope of practice

Hmm... safely and effectively... no vigorous body work or role play then. And if we go on down this failure road:

> - *you failed to* understand the need to maintain high standards of personal conduct

Did you perhaps fail to adopt and live consistently from the set of cultural values that enable the HPC to present itself as a benign protector that hides the duress which shapes its actions, i.e. no exploratory life-style innovation?

> - *you failed to* understand the importance of maintaining your own health

Well yes... except that ill health is relative and often genetically driven, and stressors such as the strong un-negotiated external demands that the HPC entails contribute, as teachers and social workers have found, to undermining health and morale.

> - *you failed to* understand both the need to keep skills and knowledge up to date and the importance of career-long learning

I.e. you may have failed to appreciate that deep in the ideological base of the HPC's approach to regulation is the notion that anything can be reduced to a set of behavioural descriptors. Psychotherapy and counselling are no exception. Not understanding the behavioural descriptors is one thing, not appreciating what is left out, empathy, intuition, nuance, relationship, lived experience, mêtis, touch and emotionality is potentially disastrous. As I have said elsewhere[2] this amounts to the systematic elimination of love by the HPC.

We might conclude this excursion into failure by noting that it could be tempting for practitioners with a humanistic and transpersonal worldview to be very even-handed and acknowledge that in its impersonal detachment this document merely reflects the perceptions of others, an aspect of the diversity of the psychological therapies. This would be a mistake since there is a clearly identifiable cluster of institutions seeking to impose a medical, university psychology, behaviourist paradigm of coercion and control. This behaviourist fundamentalism goes to the heart of the fallacy of the HPC concept of therapy as something external to the client (now patient), to be "done to them" as part of the "treatment".

While this section of generic requirements applies to all HPC registrants, there is an add-on for Psychotherapists & Counsellors:

> *they must - recognise the obligation to maintain fitness to practise including engagement in their own counselling or psychotherapy based process in a way consistent with their own theoretical approach*

> *they must - be able to identify and manage their personal involvement in and contribution to the processes of therapy, including recognising their own distress or disturbance and by being able to develop self-care strategies*

What would a failure to engage in your own 'counselling or psychotherapy based process' look like? How much supervision would you have had to miss or ignore? How often and for how long would you have to engage in personal therapy? Again, consider what would constitute failure?

Even a modest amount of contact with the evolution of the HPC and the collection of professions that it regulates points to it being something that the NHS needs, stronger than that, *has* to have.

The standards of proficiency are very obviously shaped by an NHS, i.e. a thoroughly medical approach. The medical paradigm of pathology, diagnosis, and treatment stands behind almost everything that you must be able to do, to understand, to recognise and be aware of.

And in 1b.1-b4 this NHS context comes out into the open

> **1b.1** *You must* **be able to work, where appropriate, in partnership with other professionals, support staff, service users and their relatives and carers.**

Oh yes and to go on, even if you are one of the 70 per cent or thereabouts of practitioners who don't work in the NHS:

> - *you must* understand the need to build and sustain professional relationships as both an independent practitioner and collaboratively as a member of a team

And even if you have actively rejected a medical mental illness approach to working with clients:

> - *you must* understand the need to engage service users and carers in planning and evaluating diagnostics, treatments and interventions to meet their needs and goals

They left out recognising 'pathologies' here but we'll come to it later. Remember these are legally binding requirement on registrants who sign up to them.

Also under 1b.1 there is an add-on for counsellors and psychotherapists:

> - *you must - understand the role of the therapist in the broader social and cultural context*

A very necessary requirement, not least in divining in a legally binding context what such a sentence means. Again, what would failure look like? Might this requirement imply deference? For instance, to how power is expressed in and around organisations such as the NHS, the DoH, NICE and the HPC? Understanding the role of the therapist would appear to require suppressing any sense that a coercive, duress-laden cultural context might be antipathetic to the commonplace values of psychotherapy and counselling practice, i.e. what you would actually do in the room with clients.

*- you must be able to demonstrate sensitivity to organisational dynamics*

Again a requirement that perhaps derives from NHS needs. Might it also imply that deference to existing pecking orders should be maintained – that clinical psychologists and counselling psychologists with Ph.Ds who are on salary level 11 should be acknowledged as privileged in the NHS and other hierarchies over MA/MSC psychotherapists on level 7, and no-degree counsellors on level 5. This despite extensive research which shows that para-professionals do as well with clients as highly degreed professionals; due, it might be expected, to their capacity for being present as persons rather than being present as an item of job description.

This NHS multidisciplinary team theme continues in 1.b2 where 'effective and appropriate skills in communication' must be demonstrated.

At the end of this section there is the anodyne requirement that Psychotherapists and Counsellors

*must - be able to build, maintain and end therapeutic relationships with clients*

Missing is the notion for many practitioners that therapeutic relationships are always co-created. And how curious that other essential aspects of client work are missing, remembering to collect your fee, paying into the bank, keeping records for the IR… and being sure to always change your socks every day!

In the next section, the medico-scientific ideological position of the HPC becomes more transparent. Therapy is about 'identification and assessment of health (i.e. mental health) and social care needs'.

**2a.2** *You must* **be able to select and use appropriate assessment techniques**

*You must* - be able to undertake and record a thorough, sensitive and detailed assessment, using appropriate techniques and equipment

Counsellor and psychotherapists only:

*You must - be able to devise a strategy and conduct and record the assessment process that is consistent with the theoretical approach, setting and client group*

*You must - be able to observe and record clients' responses and assess the implication for therapeutic work*

**2a.3** *You must* **- be able to undertake or arrange investigations as appropriate**

**2a.4** *You must* **- be able to analyse and critically evaluate the information collected**

*You must - be able to apply a chosen theoretical approach to assess the clients' needs*

> *You must - be able to apply a chosen theoretical approach to assess the suitability of the therapy offered to clients*

The problem with this, as elsewhere, alongside what this ideological stance demands, is what it leaves out. There is later window dressing about 'the chosen theoretical approach', no doubt due to representations from the PLG, but even then, ideological arrogance (and ignorance) shines through in the 'power over' supposition that therapy is something that is *applied* to clients: A paradigm of entering into a relationship based on rapport, support and challenge, and often the long-term waiting and listening for the emergence of a hidden client story is missing. A Gestalt approach would jointly enquire in a co-created process how the client creates and dissolves his/her preferences or expectations. Making an 'assessment' is problematical since it will impose the therapist's preferences or expectations rather than have them be an ingredient in the enquiries.

On page 7 of the draft standards there is an open embrace of NHS-manager speak in the service of a medico-scientific approach to civic accountability.

> **'Formulation and delivery of plans and strategies for meeting health and social care needs'**

Again the medical notion that it is mental health that the standards are talking about is submerged.

> **2b.1** *You must* **be able to use research, reasoning and problem solving skills to determine appropriate actions**
>
> *You must* - recognise the value of research to the critical evaluation of practice
>
> *You must* - be able to engage in evidence-based practice, evaluate practice systematically, and participate in audit procedures
>
> *You must* - be aware of a range of research methodologies
>
> *You must* - be able to demonstrate a logical and systematic approach to problem solving
>
> *You must* - be able to evaluate research and other evidence to inform [*your*] own practice

The positivist view of research in which a passive object is acted upon by an alienated enquirer who is subject to random controlled trials and statistical analysis of data is uncritically embraced here. As though this pharma-driven evidence-based practice driven approach to enquiry had not been subject to decades of critical review and challenge out of which has arisen the notion that therapy is itself a valid form of research, the outcome of which is significant *if the client experiences it as significant.*

After 2b.2, a list of anodyne specifics for counsellors and psychotherapists, we hear more of the management paradigm:

> **2b.3** *You must* **be able to formulate specific and appropriate management plans including the setting of timescales**

"Management plans" is again NHS-speak, along with the need for "timescales" irrelevant to self-employed majority of practitioners. And below in 2b.4, "treatment" is medical, "done to" stuff.

> **2b.4** *You must* **be able to conduct appropriate diagnostic or monitoring procedures, treatment, therapy or other actions safely and skilfully**

Another long list of 'musts' for counsellors and psychotherapists follows. No one seems to have noticed that some tend to be somewhat or very contradictory of the previous demands, for example:

> *You must - be able to establish an effective, collaborative working relationship with the client*
>
> *You must - be able to initiate and manage first and subsequent counselling/psychotherapy sessions by developing rapport and trust*

Again, from a non-medical humanistic, educational, gestalt, or transpersonal approach, to name only a few, we don't "manage" sessions. We might facilitate or introduce some other more collaborative, consensual approach. We might use words like "holding" or "being present" instead. And in 2b.4 there is an assumption that the practitioner *establishes* the relationship, ditto "developing rapport and trust". The client might have a difficulty with trusting people or trusting life: so how on earth does the therapist become responsible for establishing trust with them?

Another couple of musts:

> **2b.5 be able to maintain records appropriately**
>
> *You must* - be able to keep accurate, legible records and recognise the need to handle these records and all other information in accordance with applicable legislation, protocols and guidelines
>
> *You must* - understand the need to use only accepted terminology in making records

No listing of what would be accepted terminology appears, and acceptable to whom? The mind boggles at the encyclopaedic extent of what would be required! However, if sadly you should find yourself up before a 'fitness to practise' hearing, keep in mind, as a recent case demonstrated, that what might seem to you adequate notes in terminology which matches the nuances, style, spaces and *omissions* of the work you do, could be grounds for sanctions if they aren't in the legally required (but unspecified) vocabulary.

On page 9 (only two more to go) we get to the HPC's model of quality assurance.

**Critical evaluation of the impact of, or response to, the registrant's actions**

**2c.1** you must - **be able to monitor and review the ongoing effectiveness of planned activity and modify it accordingly**

*you must* - be able to gather information, including qualitative and quantitative data, that helps to evaluate the responses of service users to their care

*you must* - be able to evaluate intervention plans using recognised outcome measures and revise the plans as necessary in conjunction with the service user

*you must* - recognise the need to monitor and evaluate the quality of practice and the value of contributing to the generation of data for quality assurance and improvement programmes

*you must* - be able to make reasoned decisions to initiate, continue, modify or cease treatment or the use of techniques or procedures, and record the decisions and reasoning appropriately

This probably all sounds very reasonable to a mind entranced by a scientised approach to validity and thus in a permanent state of genuflection to reason-based medicine and a positivist version of science. And quite insane to practitioners for whom assigning this version of rationality to the sidelines of therapeutic validity has been an developmental task.

Being part of a team some years ago developing an international manufacturing quality assurance [QA] programme, plus my experience over the past 15 years of The Independent Practitioners Network [IPN], has helped me understand how QA matched to the psychological therapies can have value. From this wider perspective the HPC's notion of QA seems an obviously archaic formulation.

The HPC approach to QA is archaic because it entails an 'inspect and reject' form of quality assurance that has long been dismissed in industry as hugely wasteful. However the HPC doesn't seem to know this. Probably they have never visited a factory making video cameras or lenses, or for that matter thermostats. In such production processes, 'inspect and reject' QA was replaced decades ago by regimes of continuous scrutiny by the personnel closest to the item being produced. As and if the process goes out of spec., immediate action can be taken by them to interrupt production before any faulty item is produced. So far as I am aware, IPN is the only example of this level of scrutiny in the psychological therapies.

No amount of shape-shifting of verbiage will prevent the QA process that the HPC embodies from being fundamentally unfit for the purpose of regulating the transferential subtleties and embodied and spiritual realities of the psychological therapies.

To move on, the PLG members appear to have negotiated some caveats local to different theoretical approaches (why is it always theoretical differences – don't any of them employ a bit of mêtis?) These all apply to checking out the client experience, which I suppose is fair enough.

However at this point the infection of government and half the UK by one or another form of audit culture begins to take over the document. Keep in mind it is an 'inspect and reject' regime, i.e. action is only taken when there is a case to answer about misbehaviour. *Misbehaviour is not prevented*, it is *punished.*

> ***2c.2** You must - **be able to audit, reflect on and review practice***
>
> *You must - understand the principles of quality control and quality assurance*
>
> *You must - be aware of the role of audit and review in quality management, including quality control, quality assurance and the use of appropriate outcome measures*
>
> *You must - be able to maintain an effective audit trail and work towards continual improvement*

Expect to see a lucrative line in trainings emerging for practitioners to learn the 'use of appropriate outcome measures', how to 'maintain an effective audit trail' and participate in quality assurance programmes following recent political fashion.

> *You must - participate in quality assurance programmes, where appropriate*

But see above, only the paradigm of 'inspect and reject' QA that the HPC mistakenly sees as a match for the psychological therapies.

As though none of the above would have any effect on how they practise, the PLG seems to have managed to get in a couple of lines about supervision, a necessary but very limited notion of what is needed to sustain the ongoing capabilities of practitioners.

> *You must - understand the need for and role of supervision*
>
> *You must - be able to make use of supervision, consistent with [your] theoretical approach*
>
> *You must - be able to critically reflect on the use of self in the therapeutic process and engage in supervision in order to improve practice*

'Self' is something to be 'used', and it is introduced as if it had the same commonplace concrete meaning as 'knife and fork'.

The last section of the HPC draft standards of proficiency for counsellors and psychotherapists is devoted to

**Knowledge, understanding and skills**

In this section the HPC sees the psychological therapies through academic spectacles (they accredit courses at around sixty UK universities) coupled with the familiar medical, mental illness emphasis seen earlier.

The musts in 3a.1 include, 'Key concepts', 'bodies of knowledge', 'health', and 'disease ', 'disorder' and 'dysfunction'.

Registrants:

> *You must* - be aware of the principles and applications of scientific enquiry, including the evaluation of treatment efficacy and the research process

There is some presumption that there is only one paradigm of science, the one that has for the moment made its home in the DoH conceptual universe.

Registrants:

> *You must* - understand the theoretical basis of, and the variety of approaches to, assessment and intervention

A paean to intellectual dominance still with no acknowledgement of the prominent role of mêtis in the psychological therapies. The PLG appears to have had a few things to say about this but they are just as intellectual in their formulation; seven sentences begin with 'understand', one with 'know about'.

Even more dubious than this academic bias is the open embrace of psychiatric, i.e. *DSM IV* notions of mental health, as though its notions of 'disorder' were an uncontroversial gold standard of the human condition and not pharma/psychiatric concoctions serving, in their country of origin the US, to structure the health insurance industry's payments and revenue.

> **Psychotherapists & Counsellors (3a.1)**
>
> *You must - be able to recognise severe mental disorder in clients / or - be able to recognise disorder of the mind in clients*
>
> *You must - understand and be able to work with common / general mental health problems / or – understand and be able to work with mild / moderate mental health problems*
>
> **Psychotherapists only**
>
> *You must - understand typical presentations of severe mental disorder*
>
> You must - *understand methods of diagnosis of severe mental disorder appropriate to the theoretical approach and be able to conduct appropriate diagnostic procedures*
>
> *You must - understand and implement treatment methods to address symptoms and causes of severe mental disorder*

Counsellors appear to be seen as poor relatives who can't be trusted to get down to the nitty gritty with clients; their 'musts' are less onerous.

**Counsellors only**
*You must - understand theories and research on mental health and well-being and obstacles to wellbeing and be able to use these to facilitate client development*

*You must - understand theory and research concerning specific life problems, issues and transitions that commonly lead individuals to seek counselling and be able to use these to inform practice*

There is a bottom of the page caveat to the effect that "the views of stakeholders should be sought during the consultation process on alternative forms of wording for these 'standards" in 3a.1., as though it was only a 'wording' rather than a paradigm problem. Not surprising then that as of the end of July the BACP chair made a public rejection of the PLG recommendation that provides for separate titles and thresholds of entry for 'Psychotherapist' and 'Counsellor', plus we should add, different NHS pay scales.

Lastly the consultation document on standards and proficiency pays lip service to diversity:

**3a.2** *You must* - **know how professional principles are expressed and translated into action through a number of different approaches to practice, and how to select or modify approaches to meet the needs of an individual, groups or communities**

The text goes on to run the HPC version of the national cultural obsession with 'safety', failing to notice how this is likely to contribute to a generally risk-averse practice, as if this were in clients' interests.

**3a.3 understand the need to establish and maintain a safe practice environment**

*You must* - be aware of applicable health and safety legislation, and any relevant safety policies and procedures in force in the workplace, such as incident reporting, and be able to act in accordance with these

*You must* - be able to work safely, including being able to select appropriate hazard control and risk management, reduction or elimination techniques in a safe manner in accordance with health and safety legislation

*You must* - be able to select appropriate protective equipment and use it correctly

*You must* - be able to establish safe environments for practice, which minimise risks to service users, those treating them, and others, including the use of hazard control and particularly infection control

Here endeth the lesson, a curious form of employer-led theology that the HPC would have us absorb – that it is possible to make people moral through the use of threat, coercion and duress.

---

1 Administering The Kiss of Death – A Vichy Moment http://ipnosis.postle.net

2 Validity In the Psychological Therapies - Why Love Provides a Better Benchmark Than Science: video
http://www.veoh.com/search/videos/q/postle+love+validity#watch%3Dv178707762pAtFWfW

This and **DENIS POSTLE's** two other contributions to this collection first appeared on *e*lpnosis, a web site devoted to ways and means of holding civic accountability for clients. A collection of material from the first ten years of *e*lpnosis was published in 2006, in his *Regulating the Psychological Therapies: From Taxonomy to Taxidermy* (PCCS Books).

# State Regulation of the Psychological Therapies – ENDGAME?

Denis Postle

*A partial and not altogether even-handed review of the Health Professions Council Professional Liaison Group (PLG) Recommendations.*

**Preamble**

What kind of future might there be for the psychological therapies if the HPC succeeds in bringing them into their professions zoo? An otherwise lengthy trawl through this 'consultation' document to divine, through examining its entrails, an answer to this question, has been handily truncated by the BACP's recent refusal to run with one of its major features: that state regulation takes the form of two qualitatively distinct titles 'psychotherapist' and 'counsellor'.

It is as though the PLG in their collaboration with the HPC had gone into a meadow that had grown freely for half a century and decided that in future only two kinds of the grass found there labelled, in traditional UK style, 1st and 2nd class, were to be considered legitimate. However, if it is true, as a BACAB executive has claimed, that his organisation had accredited over 100,000 counsellors and counselling skills participants, it turns out there was a lot more counselling wheat than psychotherapy barley in the field.

Be that as it may... the BACP recently mailed its membership[1] with a request for support in persuading the HPC to reject this differentiation in the recommendations we are considering. In a break from long-standing habit, the BACP, perhaps seeking to maintain a position of executive reasonableness, has asked its membership to give the various ruling psy elites a public 'no'.

The BACP action quite possibly banjaxes psychological therapies regulation for the foreseeable future. Though they have staked out their opposition, the psychotherapists, pained to see so much hard work wasted, might concede that there is a spectrum of 'counsellotherapy' but I can't see the HPC, when they come down from the wall, agreeing to either a single or a joint title. What would it be?

So bearing all this regulatory uproar in mind, what is worth saying about the PLG recommendations? The Standards of proficiency is a much more potently insidious document, see my complementary review of it – *Scorpion Rising.* In the latter I presumed that I was writing for practitioners who have a considerable level of ambivalence and concern about the oncoming HPC regulation – if this describes you, what might you need to know about all these shenanigans?

I suspect the best I can do is to supplement the Standards review with some gleanings from the very transparent HPC PLG recommendations, and the not-so-transparent human relationships that powered them.

**The Professional Liaison Group**

First, what is the Professional Liaison Group [PLG] that has 'recommended' the future form and scope of the psychological therapies? In characteristic fashion the HPC called for nominations, then chose several layers of people; seven represented the main stakeholders, with ties to BACP, BPC, BABCP, BACAB, COSCA, Relate et al. Obvious choices perhaps. Then there was the less obvious, even arbitrary layer of four people who seemed chosen for reason of geography, leverage and reputation, Professors Fonagy and Cooper, J. Coe and J. MccMinn. A further layer of four, including the chair, could be seen as in-house HPC ballast to steady what has proved to be a predictably unstable raft. Lastly there were two 'lay' persons whose lay status was apparently legitimated by them being members of the HPC council.

The PLG was gathered together to make 'recommendations' about how the psychological therapies should be brought into state regulation. They met five times, not long to reconfigure 100 years of psychopractice. And not, as PLG members discovered at the first meeting,[2] *whether* they should be regulated. This exclusion of checking out the field's willingness to be regulated by the HPC excluded discussion of what might turn out to be a prescient element in the White Paper:

That whether or not the HPC could regulate the psychological therapies should depend on whether:

> **its system is capable of accommodating them.**

Which for many practitioners is no longer an open question.

How so? The PLG Recommendations document, in its stiff statutory style, tells us:

> 3. We undertook work to explore the statutory regulation of psychotherapists and counsellors in light of the conclusions of the White Paper.

Anyone who has followed the progress of the PLG deliberations in any detail might see the word 'explore' as economical with the truth. The Recommendations document conceals fairly successfully the extent to which the PLG was a willing collaborator in the quite brutal forcing through of an HPC-defined agenda.

If you are trying to decide how to respond to the prospect of being state regulated you might perhaps beware of getting lost in the detail of the Recommendations, much of which is more relevant to training and educational establishments than individual practitioners. Suggestion: keep your eye on the extent to which force, i.e. duress and coercion, is the cultural style of the HPC you would be signing up to.

A series of reports in *e*Ipnosis and HPCWatchDog have detailed the quality and content of the PLG's five meetings. Now we have their output. Some 31 A4 pages.

Recommendations to the HPCouncil who in turn will consider the recommendations and pass them to the DoH lawyers to turn into a legislative amendment.

These documents are freely, though not that easily, available via the HPC website. I often wonder how many people apart from those paid to do the work actually ever look at them, let alone study them carefully. It's not surprising they aren't much read, the texts often seem to bear the same relation to the PLG's reality as someone who, when asked how they are, reads a dated and timed diary of what they did in the last week – in the HPC's tightening grasp aimed at the seizure of control of the psychological therapies, everything that matters slips through their fingers.

**Education and training**

The PLG was tasked with making recommendations on the following key aspects of regulation:

Protected titles
Transfer of registers
Levels of entry to the register
Grandparenting period

Following the earlier observation that the Standards of proficiency are a more important window into what the HPC is up to, in this review I intend stepping over most of the HPC's précis of the PLG discussions to look at section 8. Education and training, and to end by pointing to a couple of anomalies, plus some remarks about the Consultation 'questions'.

Education and training tends to be a boring out-of-reach area of regulatory activity but for the future of the psychological therapies it is perhaps the most important section of the Recommendations. If state regulation of the psychological therapies is installed, dozens of training businesses, and not a few universities, stand to gain more than anyone else.

Following the PLG's recommendation of their draft Standards of proficiency for counsellors and psychotherapists, section 8.1 of the PLG recommendations introduces the approval of education and training programmes based on these standards.

> 8.1.2. The HPC visits education and training providers to approve pre-registration education and training programmes against the standards of education and training.
>
> 8.1.3. The HPC programmes [are] delivered by Higher Education Institutions (HEIs), professional bodies and private providers. There is no requirement for an approved programme to be delivered or validated by a HEI.

The spectacles through which the HPC sees this provision can be seen from the huge number of institutions with courses for the HPC-regulated healthcare professions that are presently accredited/visited. All of which, we may surmise, pay them for the endorsement. More on this below.

Later in section 8 we get to the conditions that might be thought to power the business dynamo driving state regulation.

> 8.1.7. If a programme is approved (having met any conditions if applicable), it is granted open ended approval subject to ongoing checks that the programme continues to meet the requisite standards via the annual monitoring and major change processes.
>
> 8.1.8. The HPC does not undertake cyclical re-visits of programmes (i.e. every five years).
>
> 8.1.9 …Once a programme is approved, someone who successfully completes that programme is eligible to apply for registration.
>
> **8.1.1 Opening of the Register**
>
> 10. The HPC will approve all those education and training programmes, historic and current, that led or lead to registration with one of the voluntary registers that transfers.

It is easy to see why anyone dancing in the cascade of training/supervision/supervisees/trainees business would welcome state regulation as something that consolidates their hold on this work.

While reviewing this section of the PLG report I coincidentally happened to open the HPC Approvals and Monitoring Annual Report that I had picked up on a visit to Kennington Park Road. This has a training establishment visit schedule which reveals the scale of the educational approval that the HPC presently handles. The Approvals and Monitoring Annual Report for 2006 lists HPC approved courses at around 80 universities and higher education institutions in the UK. A huge web of mutual dependence entailing considerable standardisation and bureaucratisation.

Also hidden in the HPC's quasi-legal presentation of the PLG recommendations is an intriguing circularity.

> 8.11. The Health Professions Order 2001 does not provide the HPC with a power to set the qualifications required for entry, but enables it to approve qualifications which meet the standards it has set for entry to the Register.

A wonderfully obtuse and elastic definition. And unless I am mistaken, an example of positive feedback – the Standards (again, see the review of them) come to determine what can be approved and by default what is not in the standards will be likely to be neglected (students won't want to pay to study something the HPC has no interest in). By positive feedback I mean that the more there is of certain approved elements of training, the more there will be of them and the less of what can safely be neglected. Isn't this a recipe for mediocrity and the suppression of innovation?

It also seems likely that a new training has to be born fully-formed, i.e. with HPC approval, otherwise it won't attract students. Not a problem for existing institutions with sufficient resources to get on the merry-go-round, but an obstacle, surely, to innovation.

This perspective on the HPC's effect on the future of the psychological therapies may be received as excessively rhetorical; and of course prophecy, especially with respect to the future, has a dubious record, but this is how the PLG recommendations look to me.

Let's end this review with one or two other items of interest. Here is an uncharacteristically opaque paragraph from the PLG recommendations:

> **3.3.1 Terms of reference**
>
> 14. The White Paper also said that the Government was planning to introduce statutory regulation for 'other psychological therapists'. The regulation of other occupational groups delivering psychological therapies was not directly within the PLG's terms of reference.

This seems a very cryptic statement. Who are these '*other psychological therapists*'? And the regulation of '*other occupational groups delivering psychological therapies*' was not *directly* within the PLG's terms of reference?

Another area of unsettledness that may affect many practitioners is the following discussion:

> 4.4.1
>
> 33. A smaller number of titles would be protected. For example, the 'stem titles' 'counsellor' and 'psychotherapist' might be protected. As the stem would be protected, this would cover usage of these titles as part of an adjectival title. For example, someone using the title 'psychodynamic' in front of psychotherapist would need to be registered.
>
> 4.4.2 Discussion
>
> 40. The PLG also took into account that a 'generic' approach would not limit or prevent practitioners from using adjectival / other titles in order to describe their modality or field of practice. Protecting the stem titles (e.g. 'psychotherapist' and 'counsellor') would mean that both someone using the title on its own, or with a preceding adjective, would need to registered.

This seems to be in sharp contrast to the advice in a recent message from the British Psychological Society (July 2009) in response to a query about the extent to which the generic title 'psychologist', which is not one of the seven protected 'psychologist' titles, could be used with an adjective, i.e. 'humanistic psychologist'. It elicited the following reply:

> 'Once HPC regulation begins there will be nothing to stop you using the standard 'psychologist' title or that of Holistic Psychologist'. It's only the adjectival and general titles noted at the Statutory Regulation FAQ's page that will be protected and you should be able to use any other titles than these.'

So that's all right then. I can call myself a 'humanistic psychologist' without fear of a 'cease and desist' notice arriving in the post.

This review would not be complete without some mention of the consultation questions that the HPC ask. At first sight all are 'how' questions, closed questions looking for 'yes' answers. Missing – are you convinced that the planned regulation will benefit your clients? Or do you feel that the PLG adequately represented your perspective as a practitioner? Hugely controversial notions such as 'safe and effective practice' are airily attached to 'threshold level of qualification for entry to the Register'.

When we do come to open questions they are under the heading 'Impact assessment'. Here in the word 'impact' the violence of the HPC's universe leaks out. An impact assessment reflects the reality of HPC regulation of the psychological therapies being a forced marriage; to quote the title of a piece I wrote a while back, *Chickens to wed fox and live together in henhouse.* For clients, counselling and psychotherapy are about relationship, relationship from which duress and coercion is absent. We should be under no illusions that in either these impact assessment questions or in the rest of the current consultation, Michael Guthrie and his boss Marc Seale are not making an offer of equable cooperation. They both know that it is a tank they are driving.

---

1. http://ipnosis.postle.net/PDFS/BACP%20letter%2028%20July%2009.pdf

2. For an account of the first PLG meeting, see *Administering the Kiss of Death: A Vichy Moment* http://ipnosis.postle.net/pages/PLG1stMeetingReport.htm

## Appendix

EDUCATIONAL ESTABLISHMENTS RUNNING HPC APPROVED COURSES:

Guildhall School of Music and Drama
University of Abertay, Dundee
University of Chester
University of Essex
University of Nottingham
University of Lincoln
Glasgow Caledonian University
University of Hertfordshire
The Robert Gordon University
University of the West of England, Bristol
University of Bolton
Queen Margaret University College, Edinburgh
Queen Margaret University Postgraduate College, Edinburgh
University of Wolverhampton
University of Greenwich
University of Kent
University of Northumbria at Newcastle
University of Plymouth
University of Leeds
University of Hertfordshire
University of Derby
Anglia Ruskin University
De Montfort University
University of Newcastle upon Tyne
Manchester Metropolitan University
University of Huddersfield
University of Northampton
Bournemouth University
Sheffield Hallam University
Queen Margaret University College, Edinburgh
Coventry University
University of Essex
University of Lincoln
RoyalWelsh College of Music and Drama
University of Central University
Lancashire Napier University
King's College London
University of Southampton
University of Hertfordshire
University of Sunderland
Edge Hill University
Oxford Brookes University
St George's Hospital
University of Hull
Goldsmiths College,University of London
Roehampton University
Colchester Institute
University of Greenwich
University of York
Suffolk College
University of Brighton
University of Nottingham
Nottingham Trent University
Liverpool John Moores University
University of Sheffield
London South Bank University

In August 2009 the following psychoanalytic organisations circulated comments on the Professional Liaison Group [PLG] and the HPC Standards of proficiency A covering letter on the opposite pages introduces the two critiques that follow:

**Arbours Association**

**Association of Independent Psychotherapists**

**Centre for Freudian Analysis and Research**

**The College of Psychoanalysts-UK**

**The Guild of Psychotherapists**

**Philadelphia Association**

**The Site for Contemporary Psychoanalysis**

Dear Colleague,

The Health Professions Council have now published their Draft Standards of Proficiency for Psychotherapy and Counselling. Although they have been working on the proposed regulation of the talking therapies for the last three years, the Standards will surprise many therapists and counsellors. They apply more to medical processes than to therapies, and will be unrecognisable to many practitioners. Indeed, they seem to apply more to a surgical team preparing a patient for an operation than to the open-ended relationship-based work of a talking therapy. The Standards dictate that practitioners should:

- know how to operate equipment and minimise the risk of infection.
- know how to select appropriate hazard control and risk management, reduction or elimination techniques.
- have a knowledge of health, disease, disorder and dysfunction.
- be able to evaluate and implement intervention plans using recognised outcome measures.
- know how to use protective equipment.
- know how to formulate and deliver plans and strategies for meeting health and social care needs.
- understand the principles of quality control and quality assurance and conduct audits correspondingly.
- maintain an effective audit trail, participate in audit procedures and work towards continued improvement.
- be able to formulate specific and appropriate management plans including the setting of timescales.
- demonstrate a logical and systematic approach to problem solving and be able to initiate problem solving techniques.
- observe and record client's responses.
- be able to demonstrate effective and appropriate skills in communicating information, advice and instruction.
- understand the need to engage service users and carers in planning and evaluating the diagnostics, treatment and interventions to meet their needs and goals.
- understand the importance of maintaining their own health.
- know how to meet the needs of the client.

A detailed critique of the Standards is attached to this email, together with a response to the HPC Professional Liaison Group's Report on the proposed regulation of psychotherapy and counselling. Accepting the HPC Standards threatens the talking therapies with the same fate that has met other professions: practice simply becomes a technique of risk management, with the prime concern less the work undertaken with the client than the avoidance of litigation or complaint. Complaints, indeed, would be much more likely given the definition given by HPC of a 'service user': this no longer simply refers to the client, but to "anyone who is affected by the services of a registrant", including a client's relatives or spouse, thus encouraging third party complaints.

Therapists, on the HPC model, would be obliged to act in exactly the ways they may be encouraging their clients to escape from: submission to rather than questioning of internalised authority, and a conformity to socially-agreed expectations, rather then the fostering of creativity and uniqueness that therapies have traditionally aimed at. Whereas the system of values that the talking therapies have always offered was freed from the moral judgements of social authorities, it is now made to conform to exactly these moral judgements. It will no longer be psychotherapy as we know it.

All trainings in the field will, according to HPC, be obliged to meet the Standards of Proficiency, and the hearing of complaints and fitness to practice cases will use the Standards as a benchmark. Aside from the obvious problem of medicalising the talking therapies, the therapists of the future, in such a climate, may feel they are perpetually under a judgmental gaze, the private space of the therapy becoming the stage for an internalised judge or examiner. The consequences of this on therapeutic practice cannot be underestimated, and there is an irony here that many traditional descriptions of psychotherapy define it as the effort to find freedom from the internalised observer-judge that may be at the root of the client's unhappiness.

While we unreservedly support codes of ethics and practice that ensure the practitioner's accountability, we do not believe that HPC's approach is suited to our field and so urge you, should HPC regulation take place, to adopt with us a position of principled non-compliance. If enough therapists and counsellors do not register with HPC, Government will realise the enormous mistake it is making, and our field may not face such a grim future.

The PLG report can be found at: http://www.hpc-uk.org/aboutus/consultations/

# Response to the HPC Professional Liaison Group report, July 2009

From AIP, AGIP, Arbours, CFAR, The College of Psychoanalysts-UK, Guild of Psychotherapists, The Site for Contemporary Psychoanalysis, Philadelphia Association

Before detailing specific comments on the report by the HPC Professional Liaison Group on the proposed statutory regulation of psychotherapists and counsellors, it is helpful to make some general points about the report and the draft standards of proficiency which are attached to it. All of these general points have been made repeatedly in meetings with the HPC as well as in written correspondence over the last three years:

1) The Government White Paper on 'Trust, Assurance and Safety' had given the Health Professions Council the task of assessing the 'regulatory needs' of the field and 'ensuring that its system is capable of accommodating them'. These two briefs have simply not been met by the HPC consultation or by the work of the PLG. There has been both an absence of sustained rational debate on the central issues and an exclusion of critical voices, a fact which has been brought to the attention of HPC and of MPs repeatedly.

2) Many practitioners of talking therapies do not see their work as constituting in any way a health profession, and their traditions have been critical of the received notions of health, illness and wellbeing that the HPC consultation and the PLG report take as given. Despite the fact that this point has been made innumerable times, it is not reflected in either the content of the report or the standards of proficiency.

3) The view of therapy presupposed in many parts of the report and in the standards of proficiency is at odds with many traditions of therapy over the last century. Therapy is not conceived as an intervention to be applied to a patient, but rather as an activity which the patient him or herself engages in, facilitated by the therapist. It is thus not a question of the transmission of knowledge or skills from one party to another, just as it is not in any way comparable with a medical-style intervention such as the administration of a drug or any other form of predetermined procedure.

4) The report and the standards of proficiency presuppose a concept of self that is radically rejected by many schools of psychotherapy. This is the modern idea that the self is reducible to a set of skills and competencies which must be forever improved. On this model, the human

being is seen as a business which has to better itself, making it an ever more viable competitor in the market-place. Although there may be some therapists who subscribe to this view, it is totally opposed to many therapeutic traditions which base the very work of therapy on a critique of socially accepted notions of selfhood.

For these therapies, the self is not there to be 'improved' or 'bettered', but rather to allow its history to be explored, and its fractures, frustrations and disappointments to be recognised. The growth and change that may follow do not constitute an 'improvement' or 'bettering', as this would suggest a normative view of what people should be. The standards of proficiency thus presuppose the very idea of self that thousands of therapists work every day to undermine in their practice. There is thus both a contradiction and an absurdity in trying to force therapists to frame their work within standards of proficiency that uphold the very values that the therapeutic process aims to put in question.

## Comments on HPC Draft Document on the Statutory Regulation of Psychotherapists and Counsellors

### Page 6

The constitution of the PLG is described here as including "individuals representing professional bodies, education and training providers, a qualification awarding body and organisations representing the interests of service users". It is not pointed out that the choice of the 17 members rigorously excluded all those who had critical views of HPC regulation who had been nominated by their organisations or who had nominated themselves for the PLG. It was thus a highly biased collection of individuals, which also excluded the service user group the Association of Psychoanalysis Users. Instead, HPC chose the advocacy group Witness, which is funded partly by the Department of Health and which has worked closely with HPC. It is also incorrect to state that the PLG included 'organisations' representing service users, as there was only one, if Witness can be so described.

### Page 7

The report states that 'the responses to the [HPC's] Call for Ideas informed the discussion and recommendations of the PLG'. In fact there has been a remarkable failure to respond to any of the critical responses to the Call for Ideas aside from noting which groups had made which points in a previous HPC document. After this cosmetic registering of some criticisms, HPC has failed to respond in any detailed or serious way to the points made in response to the Call for Ideas. It was pointed out several times to the HPC that the PLG meetings had failed to include adequate discussion of the majority of the points that had been made.

Paragraph 19 and 20 refer to the stakeholder events held in Manchester in March 2009. There is no mention of the criticisms made of the HPC project there or of the HPC's refusal to hold a further meeting in response to the request from stakeholders and members of the public who attended and saw an absence of any engagement with the points that were made. The Manchester event was simply there as an airbrushing exercise to create the false impression that HPC had 'listened'.

**Page 8**

Paragraph 26 It is stated that 'the role of the PLG was to discuss and make recommendations about how psychotherapists and counsellors might be regulated in light of the conclusions in the White Paper'. Yet the White Paper had required the HPC to assess the 'regulatory needs' of the field and whether it was suited to 'accommodate' this field. Neither of these crucial questions was in fact taken up in any sustained or serious way by the PLG meetings, the minutes of which are publicly available.

**Page 29**

Voluntary registers to be considered for transfer to HPC require that members demonstrate a commitment to CPD. Although many therapists would accept this idea, there are also important traditions in psychoanalysis and psychotherapy which do not accept the idea of CPD. Becoming an analyst or therapist, according to these traditions, involves profound psychological change which is not the result of knowledge or anything that can be taught in a course or learning environment. Such change can be more accurately compared to losing a limb than to memorising a handbook of information. For these traditions, that is what allows the person to then be open to working with the unconscious of other people. Given this view, it makes little sense to argue that the practitioners need to update their knowledge and skills on an annual basis. This would be like making the person prove on an annual basis that their limb hadn't miraculously re-grown. These traditions also hold that the result of any serious analysis or therapy is a questioning of the vanity of human knowledge. This is completely at odds with the modern mentality of CPD in which an 'expert' is brought in to dispense the latest knowledge to those who wish to better or improve themselves. Psychoanalysis and many forms of psychotherapy do not have a cumulative model of knowledge, but rather sees the loss of knowledge as decisive. Freud, for example, said that the analyst must forget everything they know each time they see a patient. Taking this seriously, CPD would involve ensuring that the practitioner is able to not know anything. The paradoxes of this form of assessment are also well known, with clinicians feeling that they have to prove themselves to some external authority: This, indeed, is exactly the kind of dynamic that many forms of therapy aim to collapse.

**Page 32**

Point 9 Here, and at several other places in the document, there is a reference to clinicians only being able to practise 'in those fields in which they have appropriate education, training and experience'. On the surface this may seem a very reasonable obligation, but it introduces important political factors which have an impact on how the fields are defined for which such education, training and experience are relevant. There is a very real danger here that models of diagnosis and categorisation of human distress –such as that provided by DSM – will be used here as benchmarks, despite the fact that many traditions in psychoanalysis and psychotherapy have their own classificatory systems which disagree with those of DSM, or indeed, which object to the very notion of the classification of human beings into groups through the process of dividing them via external symptoms. The danger is that notions prevalent in modern healthcare, such as 'best practice', 'evidence-based research' and 'mental illness', will be used uncritically in order to tell therapists who they can and cannot work with.

**Page 35**

The document states that if a registrant's competence is called into question, the 'standards of proficiency set by HPC are taken into account in deciding whether any action is necessary'. Since the standards of proficiency proposed are so dramatically incompatible with many long established traditions in psychotherapy, it puts registrants at great risk of having their practices adversely affected by the application of frameworks which are unsuited to assess or evaluate them.

**Page 36**

There are several paragraphs here which state the requirements of certain standards of proficiency in English language to enable a therapist or counsellor to be able to practise. This is a rather absurd requirement as there is no intrinsic reason why a therapist should have to speak a certain level of English: this may be for the obvious reason that the patients they receive would wish to speak in their own mother tongue, shared with the therapist which is not English but also, and more fundamentally, because language is itself a psychological variable which will form part of the transference. If someone has been brought up by a parent who couldn't speak the language of the country they happen to be in they may well seek out later in life a therapist who clearly has difficulty speaking a language. As long as the therapist does not claim to have standards of proficiency which they do not in fact possess, it is surely the choice of the patient who they wish to speak to. Insisting on a certain proficiency in English language removes that freedom of choice from members of the public.

The Draft Standards of Proficiency can be found at:
http://www.hpc-uk.org/aboutus/consultations/

# Response to the HPC Draft Standards of Proficiency for Psychotherapists and Counsellors

from AIP, AGIP, Arbours, CFAR, The College of Psychoanalysts-UK, Guild of Psychotherapists, The Site for Contemporary Psychoanalysis, Philadelphia Association

Before providing comments on the individual standards of proficiency, it is important to make some general points which concern issues which recur repeatedly throughout this document.

1) The HPC standards have been drafted with hardly any thought as to the specificity of the talking therapies: there are references to the use of equipment, to infection control, and to the wearing of protective clothing. The fact that requirements that are obviously tailored to medical work within hospitals or NHS trusts feature so predominantly in the HPC standards begs the question of how much attention has been paid to the particularity of the talking therapies, despite the fact that the HPC has been exploring this field apparently for at least the last three years. Nearly all of the requirements would be highly controversial when applied to the talking therapies, although less so in relation to medical work carried out within the NHS.

2) The standards of proficiency presuppose a view of therapy which is contested by most major traditions in psychotherapy today. Therapy is seen as a procedure to be applied to a passive patient, and the standards suggest time and time again the image of a patient as an object being described, assessed, evaluated and acted on by a team of experts. This view completely ignores the central feature of psychotherapy: the fact that it involves a relationship between two parties, and that the main work of the therapy is conducted not by the therapist but by the patient. The patient is not a passive object who receives treatments and procedures from a therapist, but is rather the active agent in the process of therapy.

   The standards repeatedly conceive the therapeutic process as the localised application of knowledge or skills to a patient rather than seeing the dynamical relations between patient and therapist as the central component of the work.

3) The standards repeatedly presuppose a view of the self which is not accepted by most of the main traditions in psychotherapy. The self is seen as a project to be realised, as if human beings were like faulty pieces of equipment that needed to be repaired and then continually upgraded. Psychotherapists have not been the only critics of this view of human life: philosophers and social theorists have observed and commented on this contemporary view of the self over the last

three decades. On this view, the self must be continually improved and bettered, following both the old religious discourse about self improvement and the discourse applied to inanimate objects that are deemed to require continual upgrades (a well known principle of the modern economy). While there may be some therapists who adopt this view, the main traditions in psychotherapy do not see the self as something that needs perpetual improvement and bettering, but rather believe that therapy involves a recognition of the points of fracture, loss and disappointment that the new rhetoric of the self 'to be improved' tries to obscure. Growth and change are not about 'improving' or 'bettering oneself', but emerge as possibilities based on a recognition of often painful realities. Using the vocabulary of self improvement in the standards effectively makes therapists subject to the very principles that they are doing their best to challenge in their patients.

4) The standards repeatedly refer to procedures of audit, management and predetermined outcome. These terms may be applicable in most medical and business contexts, yet have little purchase for the main traditions of psychotherapy. These traditions see therapy as involving the fostering of a freedom in the patient from precisely these irrational forms of external 'audit' and 'management'. The HPC standards would thus force the therapist to do exactly what they are trying to get their patients to question and move away from. Clinically, this will produce therapists who constantly feel they are being watched, the private space of the therapy becoming the stage for an internalised judge or examiner. The consequences of this on therapeutic practice cannot be underestimated, and there is an irony here that many traditional descriptions of psychotherapy define it as the effort to free oneself from the internalised observer-judge that may be the cause of the patient's unhappiness.

## Commentary on the Draft Standards

Please note that throughout this document, for the sake of convenience, we use the term 'patient' rather than 'client' or other terms used in different traditions of psychotherapy or counselling. It is not intended to imply a passive or medicalised position, but rather that of an active agent in the therapeutic process.

### Point 1A.1

It is stated here that psychotherapists and counsellors must 'understand the need to respect, and so far as possible uphold, the rights, dignity, values and autonomy of every service user including their role in the diagnostic and therapeutic process and in maintaining health and wellbeing'. This requirement would not be accepted by a large number of practitioners. There is no reason why a therapist should respect the values of a 'service user', just as many therapists would not see it as their role to maintain the health and well-being of the patient, seeing this as in fact the responsibility of the patient. Many therapists do not see themselves as doctors or health professionals: they provide a space for a conversation about human life, rather than any kind of healthcare delivery. Similarly, many therapists would see it as a central part of the work to voice, on occasion, their own personal disagreement with the value systems of the patient. Should the Jewish therapist respect the values of the Nazi patient? The clash of value systems may in fact be a crucial instrument of change and development within a therapeutic practice. The references here to autonomy are also unclear, and may be problematic for those traditions which aim not to foster notions of autonomy in the patient, but on the contrary, to collapse them. It is also unclear what the references to the patient's role in the diagnostic and therapeutic process are meant to mean here.

**1.6**

Psychotherapists and counsellors are required here to 'understand their duty of care with regard to the legislation on safeguarding children, young people and vulnerable adults'. There is a question here of differentiating the duty of care of the healthcare professional and the responsibility of a therapist. Many therapists would believe that they certainly have a duty in relation to their clinical work, but this duty must be differentiated from the standard of notion of duty of care, especially when it concerns questions such as confidentiality.

**1A.6**

The requirement that psychotherapists and counsellors must be able 'to assess a situation, determine the nature and severity of the problem and call upon the required knowledge and experience to deal with the problem' would not be accepted by many therapists. They would disagree with this medicalised conception of their work, which is based on the idea of localised intervention: a problem is defined and a procedure deployed to act on it. For the many schools of therapy which see their work as an open-ended conversation about the problems of human life, this requirement is entirely inappropriate. It suits more those therapies which seek concrete outcomes and solutions to problems. Many therapists, on the contrary, do not believe that they are in the problem-solving business. The danger here is that healthcare models of problems and solutions are used as a benchmark to both exclude and sanction alternative therapeutic approaches.

The requirement that psychotherapists and counsellors must 'be able to initiate resolution of problems', may be applicable to a small number of therapies but is largely antithetical to the practice and ethos of most forms of psychotherapy which are not focused on the resolution of problems and do not make any such claims to the public.

**1A.7**

The requirement that psychotherapists and counsellors must 'recognise the need for effective self management of work load and resources and be able to practise accordingly' may be applicable for staff working in organisations or NHS contexts but has nothing to do with the practice of psychotherapy.

**1A.8**

The requirement that psychotherapists and counsellors 'understand the need for high standards of personal conduct' may be applicable to some therapists, but there are many traditions of therapy which highlight precisely the human nature of the therapist, and hence human weaknesses and failings. This is of course not to condone misconduct or breaches of professional boundary, but it is important as a part of the therapeutic process that the moral values of a society do not contaminate the individual value systems that can be fostered through the work of psychotherapy and counselling. The point has been made several times that psychotherapy has always offered a system of values freed from the moral judgments of recognised social authorities. Hence it makes no sense to apply these latter standards to those who undertake therapy and become therapists precisely in order to find something different.

The requirement that psychotherapists and counsellors 'understand the importance of maintaining their own health' is also inapplicable to the majority of schools of therapy. Therapists can drink, smoke and lead sedentary lifestyles just like anyone else. They do not have a duty to conform to any particular imperative of physical well-being obtaining in any particular historical period. Of course, if problems with their physical health make it impossible for them to practise, this is an altogether different question, one which all current codes of ethics and practice recognise and proscribe against.

The requirement that psychotherapists and counsellors 'understand both the need to keep skills and knowledge up to date and the importance of career-long learning' may be applicable to some therapies but is at odds with many established traditions of psychotherapy which involve an engagement with the limits of knowledge. The idea of career-long learning is part of the contemporary ideology of betterment or improvement of the self, as if the self is a project which must be realised, to allow one maximum satisfaction and efficacy in one's work. Many traditions of psychotherapy reject this view of the self, arguing that the work of therapy involves a recognition of human fracture and frustration, a recognition of the vanity of human knowledge and a profound scepticism as to the idea of a cumulative knowledge. The kind of knowledge operative in psychotherapy is unconscious knowledge rather than academic knowledge which can be simply and readily transmitted. Training in psychotherapy involves profound psychological change and it is this change that will allow the person to work with other people as a therapist. It is not about acquiring skills and knowledge, but rather about losing them, to open oneself up to another human being. The fact that this perspective is central to a large number of established traditions of psychotherapy must be recognised in any consideration of proposed standards of proficiency.

The requirement that psychotherapists and counsellors must be able to recognise 'their own distress and disturbance and be able to develop self care strategies' also supposes a view of the self antithetical to many traditions of psychotherapy. For these traditions, therapy is not about self care strategies, and the whole notion of self care has been the subject of sustained conceptual criticism. It supposes the contemporary ideology of management of the self rather than traditional views of a recognition and engagement with conflict, contradiction and fracture. The therapist here is once again put in the place of a kind of business manager whose job it is to pursue the work of risk management of the patient at the same time as a management and audit of the self. There may be some therapists who would subscribe to this view, but this is not a part of the relational person-centred version of psychotherapy that has been established in the UK for many years.

**1B.1**

The requirement that psychotherapists and counsellors 'understand the need to build and sustain professional relationships as both an independent practitioner and collaboratively as a member of a team' may well be applicable to some therapists working within the NHS but will not apply to many who work in private practice and who are clear about the importance of independence and, in some cases, not being part of a team. The internecine fighting between therapy groups over the last eighty years has meant that many therapists see it as a virtue not to work within a group, and it is precisely this independence, even solitariness, that will attract certain patients to them rather than to other practitioners who work more closely within groups. This does not mean, of course, that the practitioner is not responsible and accountable for their work, but it means respecting the value of independence both for the therapist and for their patient.

The requirement that psychotherapists and counsellors 'understand the need to engage service users and carers in planning and evaluating the diagnostics, treatment and interventions to meet their needs and goals' may be applicable to a small number of therapies offering targeted interventions, but is not applicable to the majority of therapies which offer an open-ended exploration of human life and history. Planning and evaluating diagnostics, treatments and interventions is a medical paradigm that puts the patient in the position of an object, to whom a treatment is applied. Most therapies offer no set outcome and can make no honest promise about what will happen. Furthermore, many forms of psychotherapy aim specifically not to meet the needs and goals of the patient, with the idea that needs and goals are conscious phenomena, formulated as conscious demands, and if a distinction between conscious and unconscious thinking is recognised, the therapist has an ethical obligation to listen to the patient beyond their conscious wishes and demands. This is a fundamental feature of all psychoanalytic therapies, where the idea of meeting the patient's needs and goals makes absolutely no sense. The central ethical position of a psychoanalyst, according to the most widely practised form of psychoanalysis, is the refusal of the analyst to meet the patient's demand.

**1B.2**

The requirement that psychotherapists and counsellors 'be able to contribute effectively to work undertaken as part of multidisciplinary teams' may be applicable to certain therapists working in the NHS but has no application to most private practice therapy or counselling.

**1B.3**

The requirement that psychotherapists and counsellors must 'be able to demonstrate effective and appropriate skills in communicating information, advice, instruction and professional opinion to colleagues, service users, their relatives and carers' may be applicable to certain health professionals but has little to do with the work of therapists and counsellors. There are many reasons for this. Confidentiality, for instance, means that clinicians do not broadcast their opinion, and, for most therapists, therapy is not about advice or instruction. As for communication skills, this may be important for some forms of therapy but is certainly inappropriate for others: a Freudian psychoanalyst, for example, might remain totally silent and refuse to say anything for months or even years. The specificity and particularity of different traditions of talking therapy must be respected here and the public given the choice to pursue the form of therapy they consider appropriate, regardless of whether the therapist has communication skills or not. That is why the next requirement, that therapists and counsellors be able to communicate in English to Level 7 of the international English language testing system, is absurd. There is no intrinsic reason why a therapist should have to speak any particular level of English: this may be for the obvious reason that the patients they receive would wish to speak in their own mother tongue, shared with the therapist, but also, and more fundamentally, because language is itself a psychological variable which will form part of the transference. If someone has been brought up by a parent who couldn't speak the language of the country they happened to be in, they may well seek out later in life a therapist who clearly has difficulty speaking a language. As long as the therapist does not claim to have standards of proficiency which they do not in fact possess, it is surely the choice of the patient whom they wish to speak to. Insisting on a certain proficiency in English language removes that freedom of choice from members of the public.

The many other requirements in this section involve basic misunderstandings about language, presupposing the dated and much criticised view that language is simply a medium of communication. For most traditions of psychotherapy, as well as for the human sciences in general, language is less a medium of communication than in itself a body which has effects: the act of saying something in itself may produce change and the performative aspects of language have been well studied.

The requirement in this section that psychotherapists and counsellors 'recognise that relationships with service users should be based on mutual respect and trust' would not be accepted by all schools of therapy and it is precisely, in some cases, a lack of respect and trust that will generate the development and the dynamic of the therapeutic work. There is no intrinsic reason why a patient should trust a therapist, and indeed, it has often been argued that in an ideal world the patient's attitude should be one of sustained scepticism. It is well known that unconditional trust is the best possible framework for the abuse of power and the violation of professional boundaries. There is also no intrinsic reason why a therapist should automatically respect the patient, even if they may learn to respect them as the therapy progresses. To make it a rule that one human being should respect another is an arbitrary imperative: should the Jewish therapist automatically respect the Nazi patient, for example? Note that this does not mean that a therapist should in any way mistreat a patient, an entirely different matter which is codified against in all current codes of ethics and practice of psychotherapists.

The requirement that psychotherapists and counsellors be 'able to communicate appropriately and effectively with other professionals about the client and propose therapeutic work' may be applicable to some therapists in NHS contexts but, even then, it raises serious questions of confidentiality. We find here yet again the view that runs thorough all the HPC's standards of proficiency, that the patient is an object about whom therapists and other 'professionals' may have a discourse. The characteristic of most established psychotherapy traditions is to treat the patient as a subject and not an object. The fact that this kind of requirement keeps on emerging in the HPC standards shows the centrality of the medical model which underlies it: a group of people discuss a human being as an object of medical-style interventions to be applied to them. In contrast, for most traditions of psychotherapy, the patient is an active subject with an active engagement in the work they undertake. The main work in the therapy, after all, is performed not by the therapist but by the patient.

**1B.4**

The requirement that psychotherapists and counsellors 'understand the need for effective communication throughout the care of the service user' begs the question of whether the therapist subscribes to the notion of communication and what theory of efficacy is assumed. The Freudian's complete silence, for example, may be felt as an effective communication by one patient but as a total lack of communication by another. The therapist him or herself may likewise not feel that they are in the business of communication: they may well see their work as allowing the creation of a space in which the patient can hear themselves in a new way. It is thus not a question of communicating information or knowledge to the patient. Many therapists would also see the idea of communicating information to the patient as constituting a form of suggestion and hence consolidating the place of the therapist as a kind of master in the therapy, a situation which most therapists would want to avoid.

**2**

The requirement that psychotherapists and counsellors 'be able to build, maintain and end therapeutic relationships with clients' might seem natural enough, but it once again supposes a model of therapy as something that is applied to the patient, rather than seeing therapy as the work done by the patient. It is really the work of the patient to build, maintain and end the therapeutic relationship, although the therapist will no doubt work to facilitate this to the best of their ability. This asymmetry is another feature that is consistently ignored and unrepresented in HPC's standards of proficiency, which see therapy as a set of techniques to be applied to a patient rather than an active work performed by a patient. How, after all, can a therapist be able to end relationships with clients? A moment's reflection on this requirement shows its absurdity: if therapy is a relationship between two people with all the complexities and emotions of any passionate human relationship, it would be as if a requirement were imposed on human beings in their love relationships that they be able to end them competently. There are no rules for ending a human relationship, and to pretend that there are is pure charlatanism. Rather, what is particular to psychotherapy is precisely the fact that the difficulties, the horror, the pain and the complexity of endings actually form a part of the therapeutic work, rather than being a skill to be applied to it.

**2A.1**

The requirement that psychotherapists and counsellors 'be able to gather appropriate information' may be applicable to some health professionals working in the NHS but has little to do with most practices of psychotherapy and counselling, which are not about the gathering of information.

**2A.2**

The requirement that psychotherapists and counsellors 'be able to select and use appropriate assessment techniques' may be applicable to some therapists who work within a particular diagnostic paradigm, but there are many traditions of psychotherapy which use alternative models, in particular those which see therapy as simply a human conversation. Such therapies specifically aim to avoid the objectification of a patient through 'assessing' them. This point would apply to the following requirement, that psychotherapists and counsellors 'be able to undertake and record a thorough, sensitive and detailed assessment, using appropriate techniques and equipment'. It is remarkable that this latter phrase has been included in HPC's generic standards for psychotherapists and counsellors: even the most cursory review of the field would remind the HPC that psychotherapists and counsellors do not use equipment.

The next requirement obliges psychotherapists and counsellors to 'be able to devise a strategy and conduct and record the assessment process that is consistent with the theoretical approach, setting and client group'. This may apply to some therapies but certainly does not fit the many traditions of psychotherapy that do not subscribe to the idea of an objectifying assessment and also do not accept the principle of recording and the reduction of the patient to a written record. There are also many therapists who do not accept the idea that there is such a thing as a 'client group': rather they work with each unique individual who approaches them. When one starts to make client groups out of individuals, one necessarily imposes what some may see as arbitrary classificatory structures, something which is specifically contested by certain traditions in psychotherapy which see their work as attending to specificity and uniqueness rather than inclusion in groups and classificatory schema.

The next requirement, that psychotherapists and counsellors 'be able to observe and record clients' responses and assess the implication for therapeutic work', is problematic not only in terms of the issue of recording but also as it neglects the fact that responses can be constructed retroactively and so may only 'be observed' years later within the context of the therapeutic process. Once again the HPC standards of proficiency suppose the idea of the patient as the passive unchanging recipient of therapeutic knowledge: in other words, someone who is talked about and thought about, rather than someone whose own activity constitutes the main part of the therapeutic work.

**2A.3**

The requirement that psychotherapists and counsellors 'be able to undertake or arrange investigations as appropriate' is clearly inapplicable to the field of the talking therapies, although it may have purchase within the work of an NHS health professional.

**2A.4**

The requirement that psychotherapists and counsellors 'be able to analyse and critically evaluate the information collected' is clearly inapplicable to the work of the talking therapies, showing once again the view of the patient as an organism rather than a human participant in a person-centred therapeutic process. Hardly any forms of psychotherapy would see their work as involving the collection of information, although this is of course exactly what characterises some aspects of the medical model of healthcare delivery. In therapy, the therapist does not collect information about the patient and then use it to apply a procedure to a patient. Rather, there is an ongoing dialectical relation grounded in speech, which is of course radically different from information.

The next section is entitled 'Formulation and delivery of plans and strategies for meeting health and social care needs'. The very title of this section is indicative of HPC's failure to understand the basis of most forms of talking therapy, which do not involve the delivery of plans and strategies, just as they do not involve meeting health and social care needs of patients. These paradigms belong to a medical model of health care in which a team are treating a patient with targeted intervention such as the administration of a surgical procedure, a treatment via pharmaceuticals or other forms of medical and quasi-medical process. Most psychotherapists would fail to recognise their work in the requirement that they are there to meet the health and social care needs of their patients. And in fact, most would probably see the particularity of their work as offering precisely something which did not fit within the health and social care paradigm. Trying to fit their work into this paradigm not only does an injustice to this work and to the work of many patients in therapy, but would also have detrimental effects on trainings which, as the PLG report makes clear, will have to formulate teaching to fit these standards of proficiency.

**2B.1**
The requirement that psychotherapists and counsellors 'be able to use research, reasoning and problem solving skills to determine appropriate action' may be appropriate for a minority of cognitive-based therapies but is at odds with most traditions of psychotherapy which do not see their work in terms of problem-solving skills and do not aim to formulate specific actions to respond to specific problems.

The next requirement, that psychotherapists and counsellors 'be able to engage in evidence based practice, evaluate practice systematically, and participate in audit procedures', is once again entirely inappropriate for many forms of psychotherapy, which eschew the rhetoric of evidence-based practice and believe that its ubiquity today is based on profoundly flawed premises. There is now a large literature critiquing the notion of evidence based practice, and many traditions in psychotherapy see it as of the utmost importance to distance their work from the rhetoric of evidence-based research, which of course carries the danger that – once inappropriate research 'shows' that one method of treatment is 'best practice' for a particular symptom – that other forms of therapy be excluded, thus depriving patients of the choice of working with the therapeutic process they choose. Many schools of psychotherapy, likewise, would not accept the notion of audit procedures, a practice linked to management and to the world of business or managed health care rather than to the individual and creative conversation about human life that constitutes the stuff of many forms of psychotherapy.

The requirement that psychotherapists and counsellors be able to 'demonstrate a logical and systematic approach to problem solving' once again supposes that therapists are in the business of problem solving. As we have noted several times above, there may be some forms of therapy that do, but in general this is not the case.

**2B.2**

The requirement that psychotherapists and counsellors 'be able to change their practice as needed to take account of new developments' in the area of 'knowledge and skills' is applicable to a medical-based model but not to the majority of forms of psychotherapy where the large part of the work is done by the patient, facilitated by the psychotherapist. In medicine, a doctor may learn that a drug being prescribed is harmful and may then cease to prescribe it. This would be an example of a new development informing a practice, but knowledge in psychotherapy is different from knowledge in medicine. The 'new developments' that matter in the therapy will be those that come from the patient rather than from the therapist.

The following requirement that psychotherapists and counsellors 'be able to demonstrate a level of skill in the use of information technology appropriate to their practice' is absurd and may apply to some health professionals working in the NHS, but has nothing whatsoever to do with psychotherapy and counselling.

The requirement that psychotherapists and counsellors 'be able to recognise when further therapy work is inappropriate or unlikely to be helpful' is problematic as the articulation of such a view to a patient may have catastrophic effects. Although the issues here are clearly complex, it seems likely that the formulation of this requirement is based on a medical model in which a team is responsible for the health of a patient. It also opens up the obvious question of third party complaints, as there must be tens of thousands of spouses and family members of people in therapy across the country who are convinced that the therapy that their loved one is undertaking is inappropriate and unhelpful. This is an everyday situation which therapists and counsellors are familiar with, and the particular formulation of the 'standard of proficiency' here runs the risk of implying that there are objective, externally verifiable standards of whether a therapeutic work is inappropriate or unhelpful.

The requirement that psychotherapists and counsellors 'be able to make informed judgments on complex issues in the absence of complete information' is one of the most absurd in all of the standards of proficiency. It is obviously just taken from a medical model where information may be necessary about health issues prior to the prescription of a drug or surgery. In a psychotherapy, how can information ever be complete? What sort of fantasy would either the patient or therapist have if they believed in the idea of complete information?

**2B.3**

The requirement that psychotherapists and counsellors 'be able to formulate specific and appropriate management plans including the setting of timescales' may be suited to some staff working within NHS contexts but has little to do with the open-ended work of psychotherapy which often does not have a time limit and which eschews the very idea of a 'management plan'. Since it is never possible to predict in advance what will happen in the therapy, it is clearly absurd to believe one could formulate 'specific and appropriate management plans'. While this may have a sense in the context of a targeted health-care intervention, it has little to do with the talking therapies, many of which specifically reject the concept of the 'management' of human beings. These therapies differentiate themselves from practices associated with social engineering.

**2B.4**

The requirement that psychotherapists and counsellors 'be able to conduct appropriate diagnostic or monitoring procedures, treatments, therapy or other actions carefully and skilfully' may be appropriate for a laboratory technician but not for most forms of psychotherapy. Psychotherapy does not involve the application of a procedure or treatment to a patient but is the work created by a patient, facilitated by a therapist. Very few forms of therapy involve the application of any procedure, and it is often argued that those who do in effect disqualify themselves as psychotherapies for that very reason. As noted above, many forms of therapy, likewise, would not accept the notion of diagnostic or 'monitoring procedures'. As for the reference to skills, there may be some therapists who pride themselves on performing their work skillfully, yet there are many others who give a central place to blunder, error, failing and any of the other difficulties which constitute human life. For many therapists, it is an engagement with these failings that a large part of the work of therapy is about. This would involve a questioning of ideals of both autonomy and mastery, and fantasies of one's own self image as a skilful 'expert'.

The requirement that psychotherapists and counsellors 'understand the need to maintain the safety of both service users and those involved in their care' has a very limited application for psychotherapy. The primary responsibility of the therapist is not to ensure the health of their patient but simply, for many clinicians, to allow a conversation to take place. They would obviously need to ensure that there is an appropriate fire exit from their office and that there are no dangerous obstacles which might put the client in danger of slipping or falling in the consulting room, but beyond this, most traditions of psychotherapy see the maintaining of health as a personal responsibility of the patient rather than being a duty that the therapist must take on for them.

The requirement that psychotherapists and counsellors 'be able to establish an effective, collaborative working relationship with a client' is inapplicable to most forms of psychotherapy since, for many psychotherapy traditions, psychotherapy is not something that one person applies to another, but is rather a property of the relationship between two people. Given this, it is hardly a requirement for the psychotherapist to establish an effective collaborative relationship, since a large part of this work will come from the patient. The parallel is obviously in terms of everyday relationships between people. Whether a relationship works or not does not depend on one person but on both.

The requirement that psychotherapists and counsellors 'be able to enable and work with expression of client emotion' is problematic in that there are different theories about what constitutes emotion and whether, indeed, there is any difference between emotion and the expression of emotion. There is a vast literature on this question. Some traditions of psychotherapy do not place great value on the expression of emotion, arguing instead that what matters are the unconscious thought processes underpinning emotions, which in themselves may be misleading. Other therapies do place a great emphasis on the release of emotion, but there is no consensus view on either the nature or place of emotion in the field of psychotherapy.

The requirement that psychotherapists and counsellors 'be able to communicate empathic understanding to clients' would be rejected by many traditions of psychotherapy which hold that empathy with a patient is a sign that something has gone wrong in the therapeutic process. For these traditions, there must be a certain distance established between the therapist and the patient, and, most importantly, the therapist must recognise that they can never know exactly what is going on in the patient's mind, and certainly can never claim to understand their experiences. For these traditions in psychotherapy, listening may be sympathetic and attentive but is not empathic, which would imply that the internal states of the patient are accessible and shared by the therapist. This may be experienced by the patient as a gross intrusion and a denial of the singularity of their own experience. Other traditions and therapies do of course emphasise the importance of empathy. There is no consensus on this issue in the field.

The requirement that psychotherapists and counsellors 'be able to initiate and manage first and subsequent counselling/psychotherapy sessions by developing rapport and trust' is inapplicable to many traditions of psychotherapy. For example, the Freudian who sits there in silence may not be aiming to actively develop rapport and trust with a patient, even though rapport and trust may result from the resolute maintaining of this silence. Many traditions of psychotherapy would also argue that if the therapist actively tries to make the patient trust him or her, there is something wrong with the therapeutic process. Trust should not be an automatic property of the relationship, but will rather depend on transference issues. If a patient systematically mistrusts their therapist, the reasons for this may be explored. This would be very different from the therapist trying to make themselves trusted, which can only be a symptom of the instability of their own position.

The requirement that psychotherapists and counsellors 'be able to respect and take into account the client's capacity for self determination' is problematic, given the fact that many traditions of psychotherapy see the very concept of self determination as in question. For many traditions, autonomy and self determination are fictions, often with a political agenda. For these traditions, what matters would be to explore the structures that determine the lived experience of the patient and, at the end of the therapy, it may become clear to the patient that there are profound limits to any supposed autonomy or self determination.

The requirement that psychotherapists and counsellors 'be able to work with both the explicit and implicit aspects of the therapeutic relationship' is mystifying: it is unclear what exactly this might mean.

**2B.5**

The requirement that psychotherapists and counsellors 'be able to keep accurate, legible records and recognise the need to handle these records and all other information with applicable legislation, protocol and guidelines' may be applicable to those working in the NHS and for most health professionals, but is at odds with many traditions in psychotherapy. Freud and most other subsequent psychoanalytic thinkers advised against record keeping, arguing that it blocks the spontaneity of unconscious communication between patient and analyst. It is also widely recognised that record keeping may simply serve as a way to block the therapist's anxiety, and that they would be better served by discussing the relevant issues in their own personal therapy or supervision.

The requirement that psychotherapists and counsellors 'understand the need to use only accepted terminology in making records' is absurd, as it implies that there is such a thing as accepted terminology in the field of the talking therapies: would the terminology include 'shadow', 'jouissance' 'plane of identification', 'matheme' etc.?

The danger here, as elsewhere, is that therapists will gradually begin to not only document but also think about their own practice through the eyes of someone they think is watching them, be this benevolent or malign. The moment that therapy becomes experienced in these terms, as if taking place on a stage for a third party to monitor, it ceases to be true psychotherapy, and perpetuates the very dynamic that the therapy itself may be trying to free the patient from.

**2C.1**

The requirement that psychotherapists and counsellors 'be able to monitor and review the ongoing effectiveness of planned activity and modify it accordingly' is at odds with many traditions of psychotherapy which do not plan intervention or activity, seeing therapy rather as an ongoing, creative and unpredictably unfolding conversation. It is not a question of formulating and applying specific procedures which can be monitored and checked.

The requirement that psychotherapists and counsellors 'be able to gather information, including qualitative and quantitative data, that helps to evaluate the responses of service users to their care' may be applicable to some health professionals but is at odds with most traditions of psychotherapy, which do not seek to gather information or to perform procedures of evaluation.

The requirement that psychotherapists and counsellors 'be able to evaluate intervention plans using recognised outcome measures and revise the plans as necessary in conjunction with the service user' may be applicable for some health professionals but has absolutely no application to most forms of psychotherapy. Most forms of psychotherapy do not involve the establishment of intervention plans that are then applied to the patient as the recipient of a procedure, and in most psychotherapies there is no notion of 'recognised outcome measures'. It is often argued that the difference between psychotherapy and mental hygiene is precisely this: that in mental hygiene the therapist knows what is best in advance for the patient and tries to implement this. In psychotherapy, on the contrary, the psychotherapist listens to what the patient has to say.

The requirement that psychotherapists and counsellors 'recognise the need to monitor and evaluate the quality of practice and the value of contributing to the generation of data for quality assurance and improvement programmes' is totally inapplicable to the field of psychotherapy. This is not just due to the problems with the idea of 'monitoring and evaluating' that we have discussed above, but gives the therapist the role of a bureaucrat, with the task of managing the patient rather than that of a partner in a dialogue accompanying the patient on their journey. The notion of 'quality assurance' is anathema to those traditions of psychotherapy that are not based on a business model of service provision, and the notion of an 'improvement programme' also belongs to a modern ideology of the self which most of the major traditions in psychotherapy eschew.

The requirement that psychotherapists and counsellors 'be able to make reasoned decisions to initiate, continue, modify or cease treatment for the use of techniques or procedures, and record the decision and reasoning appropriately' is at odds with most forms of psychotherapy which do not use techniques or procedures, and once again, this requirement begs the question of why every clinical decision would need to be recorded and explained. This would create a mindset in which everything the therapist did would only make sense given an observing eye that would be judging their action. This form of internalised authority may be useful in techniques such as policing but runs counter to the major traditions in psychotherapy which are about freeing oneself from the tyranny of internalised forms of irrational authority.

The requirement that psychotherapists and counsellors 'be able to help clients to reflect on their process [progress?] of therapy' is certainly applicable to many forms of psychotherapy today, but it is equally incompatible with many other forms of contemporary practice. Some forms of psychotherapy involve a continued focusing on the relation between the patient and the therapist, whereas other forms aim to open up a space beyond the consulting room and to subordinate the therapeutic process to these other variables. There is thus no consensus view on the importance or necessity of making patients reflect on the therapeutic process. This point applies to the following requirements that the therapist 'review and evaluate' their work with the patient. For many forms of therapy, it is technically a mistake to bring things back to the relation between the two parties, following one version of the object relations tradition.

The requirement that psychotherapists and counsellors 'be able to evaluate the therapeutic work in collaboration with the client' supposes once again that there is some kind of external position from which the work of therapy can be assessed and evaluated, rather than seeing it as an organic, unfolding and open-ended process. Since this process is constituted by the relation between the patient and the therapist, neither is able to abstract themselves from it to give an 'objective view' or evaluation.

**2C.2**

The requirement that psychotherapists and counsellors 'be able to audit, reflect on and review practice' would be acceptable if it was limited to the verb 'reflect on'. Psychotherapists do not audit their practice, although no doubt those who work in business or in some forms of healthcare delivery might wish to do so.

The requirement that psychotherapists and counsellors 'understand the principles of quality control and quality assurance' may be applicable to business contexts and some forms of healthcare but is largely inapplicable to most traditions in psychotherapy which do not use the conceptual vocabulary of quality control or quality assurance. The key to these traditions is precisely the fact that they offer a space outside the market place, one in which human beings are not seen as 'resources'. Most traditions of psychotherapy do not view human life as a series of business-style transactions, and they do not use business vocabulary to describe human beings.

The requirement that psychotherapists and counsellors 'be aware of the role of audit and review in quality management including quality control, quality assurance and the use of appropriate outcome measures' is absurd and inapplicable for the reasons outlined above. As has been repeated, these concepts are at odds with the ethics of most forms of psychotherapy which, likewise, do not have a notion of 'outcome measures'.

The requirement that psychotherapists and counsellors 'be able to maintain an effective audit trail and work towards continued improvement' is totally inappropriate for most forms of psychotherapy, although it may be appropriate for business contexts. Likewise, many of the major traditions in psychotherapy do not believe in the modern ideology of 'continual improvement' but rather aim to give a place to the central experiences of disappointment and frustration that lie at the heart of human life. It is precisely the well being industry that promotes the idea of 'continual improvement', often in order to sell products to the public. Most forms of psychotherapy, on the contrary, are characterised by their refusal to enter into this form of transaction, and do not make promises to the public about results or endeavour to sell products.

The requirement that psychotherapists and counsellors 'be able to critically reflect on the use of self in the therapeutic process and engage in supervision in order to improve practice' may be applicable to some forms of therapy today, but would be at odds with many traditions of therapy which do not see the self as a tool to be used in the therapeutic process, or even as any fixed entity. There are also several traditions of psychotherapy which are critical of the very notion of the 'self' and, for those who do accept it, it is not always seen as a variable that can itself be the object of reflection: this would once again suppose that the therapist could abstract themself from 'themself', precisely the kind of dissociation that the HPC framework is designed to foster. As regards supervision, although all traditions of psychotherapy give a central place to the practice of supervision, there is no general agreement that the role of supervision improves practice.

**3A.1**

The requirement that psychotherapists and counsellors 'understand the structure and function of the human body, relevant to their practice, together with knowledge of health, disease, disorder and dysfunction' may be applicable to those working in the medical field but has little to do with most forms of psychotherapy. There are some forms of therapy which do involve a focus on the body, yet these may presuppose different models of structure and function from those presupposed by mainstream medicine. Likewise, many traditions in psychotherapy do not accept the concept of health, disease, disorder and dysfunction as applied to psychological matters.

The requirement that psychotherapists and counsellors 'be aware of the principles and application of scientific enquiry, including the evaluation of treatment efficacy and the research process' is not unreasonable in the field of the talking therapies, but there is the serious danger here that it would involve a limited conception of scientific enquiry, efficacy and research. HPC and Skills for Health, for example, have very limited and monolithic notions of these variables, foreclosing completely the rich tradition in history and philosophy of science that has been developed in this country over the last hundred years. There is a grave risk that fashionable notions of scientific enquiry, efficacy and research will be used as benchmarks to evaluate therapeutic practice, rather than themselves being the object of critical enquiry in the tradition of work in the history and philosophy of science.

The requirement that psychotherapists and counsellors 'understand the typical presentations of severe mental disorder' is at odds with many traditions of psychotherapy which are critical of the very notion of mental disorder. There is the risk here that psychiatric notions of mental disorder are used as a benchmark in the evaluation of therapeutic practices when these practices may either reject classificatory systems or use alternate classificatory systems to those of psychiatrists. For example, there is massive disagreement as to the clinical signs of non-triggered psychosis, and different traditions will have radically different views as to what these signs might consist of. These concerns apply to the following requirement that psychotherapists and counsellors 'understand methods of diagnosis of severe mental disorder.... and be able to conduct appropriate diagnostic procedures'.

The requirement that counsellors 'understand theories and research on mental health and well being and obstacles to wellbeing and be able to use these to facilitate the client's development' might be applicable to some forms of counselling but not to those which are critical of the notion of well-being, which is effectively the market place today for selling products to the public. The appearance of the term here under the rubric of 'counsellors' only shows a certain disrespect to the important work that counsellors do, as if the counsellors were just concerned with well-being and the therapists were doing something different.

**3A.2**
The requirement that psychotherapists and counsellors 'select or modify approaches to meet the needs of an individual, group or community' may be applicable to a small range of therapies, but is at odds with those major traditions of psychotherapy which do not see the work of therapy as involving meeting anyone's needs. Many forms of therapy involve a questioning of what the patient feels they want, and the needs that the patient presents are, in these traditions, taken as symptoms which need deciphering rather than 'meeting'. In psychoanalysis, for example, the central ethical position of the analyst involves the sustained refusal to meet the needs of the patient.

**3A.3**
The requirement that psychotherapists and counsellors 'be aware of applicable health and safety legislation and any relevant safety policies and procedures in force in the workplace, such as incident reporting, and be able to act in accordance with these' is obviously applicable to those working in NHS contexts but hardly for therapies conducted in private practice, beyond the most obvious measures taken to ensure that the consulting room does not contain hazardous objects or, have a slippery floor, or any craters into which the patient might fall.

The requirement that psychotherapists and counsellors 'be able to select appropriate hazard control and risk management, reduction or elimination techniques' is likewise inapplicable to most private practice psychotherapy contexts, just as is the requirement that they 'be able to select appropriate protective equipment and use it correctly'.

The next requirement regarding 'hazard control and particularly infection control' is obviously inapplicable to the talking therapies. It is extraordinary that these latter requirements have been included in such an important document, after the HPC has been supposed to have been thinking about the field of talking therapies for at least three years now.

**RICHARD HOUSE** Ph.D. is Senior Lecturer in Psychotherapy and Counselling, Roehampton University. Books include *Therapy Beyond Modernity* (Karnac, 2003), and co-editing *Implausible Professions* (1997) and *Against and For CBT* (2008 – both PCCS Books). An Independent Practitioners Network founder-participant, he co-orchestrated the two *Daily Telegraph* Open Letters on 'toxic childhood' and 'play' (2006 and 2007).

HEALTH PROFESSIONS COUNCIL CONSULTATION

# The PLG's Proposals for the Statutory Regulation of Counselling & Psychotherapy

**SUBMISSION OF EVIDENCE**
Dr Richard House

## BACKGROUND

The following paper is a detailed response to the Health Professions Council's (HPC) Consultation Document on the recommendations of the Psychotherapists and Counsellors Professional Liaison Group (PLG) on the proposed state regulation of psychotherapists and counsellors. I write as a trained counsellor/therapist who has been practising since 1990, having trained in Counselling and Groupwork, and then in Body-oriented Psychotherapy, between 1987 and 1995. I am also a Senior Lecturer in Psychotherapy and Counselling at a London University which trains large numbers of psychotherapists and counselling psychologists; and I am an ongoing participant in the Independent Practitioners Network, of which I was a founding participant in 1994. I have a considerable list of professional publications on the theme of therapy regulation and professionalisation spanning nearly two decades, and a full list of these publications is appended to this paper.

## INTRODUCTION

This paper consists of several parts. I begin by arguing, *inter alia,* that:

- the state regulation of the psychological therapies has no evidence base to support it;
- there is no evidence that regulation will succeed in achieving its stated intention of 'protecting the public' any more successfully than the diverse regulatory framework that currently exists in the British 'psy' field;
- there is both anecdotal and research evidence to suggest that net harm might well be perpetrated upon the therapy field as a whole by state regulation; and that
- by implementing these proposals without any detailed research or consultation with actual practitioners (as opposed to unrepresentative professional interest groups) into the 'general equilibrium effects' of these changes, the Government is effectively playing Russian Roulette with the future quality of therapy work in the UK, and is intruding into a sphere into which it is illegitimate for the state to intervene.

In short, ***there exists no rational case whatsoever for the state regulation of the psy therapies***; and it follows that if such regulation does go ahead, it will be being driven by political or politician-centred expediency, vested (economic) training interests and empire-building, and/or paradigmatic (modernist) influences, none of which have little if anything to do with rational argumentation. As Mowbray wrote 15 years ago (and little has changed since then), '...the main impetus [towards regulation] seems to have been coming from a rather small nucleus of people within the movement (many with a vested interest in training)' (Mowbray, 1995: 20).

On this view, HPC state regulation (hereafter, SR) is a quite unwarranted and inappropriate use of state power, in a field that has actually been remarkably successful and effective in regulating itself over many decades (I return to this later). It is also totally unacceptable that the many thousands of practitioners who, like myself, have spent literally thousands of pounds of their own money on training over many years are now being subject to changes in our work that many believe will have far-reaching, long-term negative consequences, and about which there has been no systematic attempt to survey psy practitioners on the ground regarding their views on regulation.

Moreover, following the socio-cultural cosmology articulated a century ago by Rudolf Steiner in his highly progressive 'Threefold Social Order' notion (returned to later), the realms of both health care (broadly defined) and education (also broadly defined) should be located within the free cultural sphere of society, and not within the political sphere, which should essentially confine itself to the themes of human rights and equality before the law. The kinds of innovation and creativity that are essential in the psychological therapies (cf. the collections edited by House and Totton, 1997; Bates and House, 2004) if this kind of healing practice is to evolve can only be compromised when SR cements in place an institutionally professionalised therapy practice that can then so easily become *a status quo practice*, that reinforces *what is*. Put differently, therapy work is subtle, highly complex, and in many ways *ineffable*; and by its very nature, the state is quite unable effectively or appropriately to regulate or administer an activity of this nature.

Thus, a major 'category error' is therefore being perpetrated in this SR proposal, and my intention in this paper is to articulate in as much detail as necessary the nature of this category error. This latter will entail a detailed critique of the positivist, 'modernist' worldview that (unwittingly?) underpins these proposals, and the inappropriateness of 'shoe-horning' what is, for many practitioners, a non-positivistic, post-modern healing practice into an alien framework whose assumptions do a kind of violence to the nature of our work.

The adoption of a *standardisation ideology* also betrays the 'modernist' worldview that is informing those who are planning to state-regulate our activity. It is the crucial post-modern and transpersonal subtleties and nuances of our activity that the standardisation-obsessed policy-makers and state regulators seem either quite unable to grasp, or else are determined wilfully to ignore. This struggle is part of a wider 'paradigm war' in modern culture, between the forces of late modernity, on the one hand, and trans- or postmodernity, on the other.[1]

In sum, the ideology of standardisation is just that, then – an ideology rooted in a normalising, late-modernist worldview that, for many if not the majority of therapists, is fundamentally to misunderstand, misrepresent and even do a kind of violence to core therapy values, which at their best are striving to transcend the crude bludgeon of late modernity. I have argued at length elsewhere (e.g. in *Therapy Beyond Modernity*, House, 2003) that at its best, therapy is a 'post-professional' practice in the sense articulated by the late Ivan Illich; yet SR cements in place a self-interested and self-perpetuating 'profession' which will tend to reinforce the profession-centred identity of psy work. Again, I return to this crucial issue later in this paper.

Writing this paper also demands great clarity, as it would be all too easy to engage critically with the PLG's draft 'Standards of Proficiency' (SoP), and thereby give the impression that the *principle* of SR is acceptable and legitimate, and only the detailed minutiae need some fine-tuning. So to be clear and unambiguous at this point: **the principle of SR is fundamentally flawed and inappropriate for the psy field, and it is this inappropriateness which generates many if not most of the absurdities in the SoP, as set out in the consultation document** (and which will be detailed below in section 5). Thus, when I critique the latter, I am not in any way arguing that a response to those criticisms would somehow render SR acceptable and appropriate. My strong view, held over many years, is that the state regulation of the psy therapies (whether via the HPC or in any other way) is inappropriate and wrong-headed, and no degree of tinkering with the language or the substance of the 'proficiency standards' can change this fact.

In section 2 of this paper, I present a summary of the general arguments as to why the SR of the psychological therapies is inadvisable and contra-indicated.

**Section note**

1 See, for example, M. Woodhouse, *Paradigm Wars; World Views for a New Age*, Frog, Calif., 1996; and R. Tarnas, *The Passion of the Western Mind: Understanding the Ideas that Have Shaped Our World View*, Ballantine, New York, 1993.

## 2 WHY STATE REGULATION IS FUNDAMENTALLY AND NECESSARILY FLAWED

While this paper is not primarily concerned with the broad generic arguments against SR, it is important to summarise those arguments, as a contextualising backdrop to the rest of this paper.

There is a large number of compelling reasons for opposing HPC-based regulation of the psychological therapies. First, and perhaps most telling, the detailed argumentation that would be required to make any kind of case for regulation by a state-sponsored body has never been made, but it is simply and repeatedly asserted and assumed, despite repeated requests from regulation's critics for those favouring regulation to provide a fully articulated 'case for' regulation. Consequently, many practitioners dispute on both theoretical and practical grounds the HPC regulatory regime currently being threatened.

Moreover, essentially the only rationale that is ever proposed by the pro-regulation constituency is that of 'protection of the public'; indeed, on page 1 of its consultation document, for example, the HPC states unambiguously that 'our job is to protect the health and wellbeing of people who use the services of the professionals registered with us'. And on p. 24 of its recommendations document, the PLG writes that 'failure to protect the title [of counsellor] would risk large evasion of regulation and *therefore reduce the level of public protection*' (italics added). On p. 28, we read that 'The PLG agreed that the criteria set [for voluntary register transfer] should be those necessary to *ensure* public protection' (italics added). Notice here, as elsewhere, that the view that regulation will somehow enhance the net level of public protection is merely asserted, never *argued* in anything approaching a coherent or thorough way. I submit, and will argue at length below, that this lacuna in the 'case for' regulation is because the 'argument' that regulation will enhance public protection is essentially threadbare.

Thus, in the following detailing of the arguments against regulation, therefore, I will do what the pro-regulation lobby has consistently failed to do, and give particularly concerted attention to the argument that SR will enhance 'protection of the public', in a comprehensive refutation of that highly dubious and consistently unsubstantiated claim.

First, there exists no systematic research evidence demonstrating widespread levels of abuse by practitioners that exceeds that seen in any number of other fields, and which could therefore be argued to require special legislative intervention. Tellingly, in a recently published pro-regulation article, Jonathan Coe of Witness cited empirical research data based on just one British survey of *clinical psychologists'* abusive behaviour *conducted about 20 years ago*, and on data from the USA from Pope and Vetter *published in 1991*, in his attempt to make the case for regulation! This strongly suggests that the drive to state-regulate is based on little more than knee-jerk anecdote alone. Indeed, it could be convincingly argued that it is the very taking of responsibility for ethical practice by the (until now) self-regulating psy field itself, in all its rich diversity, which has been a major factor in the comparatively low levels of abuse observable in the psy field. For it is quite demonstrably a self-regulating framework for the psychological therapies through various professional bodies that has contributed to a field of richness, innovation and diversity over several decades – so if it ain't broke, why on earth try to fix it? Moreover, despite repeatedly being asked to come up with reputable data on the level of abuse in the psy field in Britain, the Department of Health has failed to do so. It would be relatively easy to research into this area, and to produce reasonably robust data upon which to base policy in an informed way – if, of course, the political will existed to do so.

The *nature* of abuse in the psy field is also subtly but significantly different from abuse in other fields, and therefore requires a distinctive response. In psychotherapy relationships, the nature of what constitutes genuine abuse and legitimate complaint is highly complex when, *by the very nature of the work*, the practitioner lays him- or herself open to negative projections and 'biographical re-enactments' from the client. Indeed, as Mowbray, quoting Stanislav Grof, states: 'the intensity of what are regarded as symptoms under the medical model is actually an indication that a healing and transformative process is at work' (Mowbray, 1995: 103); and quoting Danial B. Hogan: 'What constitutes... deterioration depends on how psychotherapy is conceived' (ibid.: 101). Yet the only kind of disciplining regulation that the HPC and the state seem capable of 'delivering' is of the legalistic, 'managerialist' kind, that polarises around the simplistic discourse of innocent/guilty, and which therefore necessarily rides rough-shod over the subtleties and complexities of this delicate and unique kind of work. Moreover, the lack of objective or universal benchmark consensus regarding outcome and ethics is an absence which is *intrinsic to the activity*, and which therefore leaves these activities especially vulnerable to pernicious complaints. Mowbray again, quoting Michael Trebilcock and Jeffrey Shaul: 'If ignorance about what is a good or bad outcome, or what is good or bad procedure, is... pervasive..., then... no settled bench marks can be identified upon which to base any regulatory strategy directed to promoting service quality' (Mowbray, 1995: 148); and it is perpetrating a fraud on the public to pretend that it is rationally and procedurally possible to do so.

It has been argued, further, that laws restricting a person's right to pursue an occupation should not be enacted unless, in a linear-causal sense, 'practitioner incompetence [can] be shown to be the source of harm' (Mowbray, 1995: 91). Yet (Mowbray), '...it is by no means inevitable that… potential for abuse lies in the practitioner's favour. Such a view assumes that the situation is seen through the lens of a medical model' (ibid.: 111). According to Daniel B. Hogan, 'the lack of consensus as to what causes danger and how to measure it should prevent the enactment of laws restricting a person's right to practise... [F]actors quite apart from the practitioner, such as the initial level of a patient's mental health, may account for a large share of the harm that occurs in therapy' (quoted in ibid.: 108).

The pursuit of regulation and licensing to reduce client abuse also uncritically presupposes that registered practitioners are less likely to commit abuse than are unregistered ones. Yet according to Mowbray, 'there is no clear evidence to [indicate] that [the] incidence [of abuse] differs between licensed and unlicensed settings' (Mowbray, 1995: 112); and the cases of abuse perpetrated by therapists referred to by Jeffrey Masson in his book *Against Therapy* 'mainly involved practitioners who were already licensed professionals (i.e. medical doctors, clinical psychologists), and their resulting status in the community if anything made it *harder* to challenge their abuses' (ibid.).

In terms of legitimate and appropriate client redress, as Mowbray (1995: 154) argues, the seeking of redress of a punitive nature via a legalistic framework 'is rarely appropriate for an activity whose stock in trade is "unfinished business" of an emotional nature. Encouraging a settlement on the level at which the problem exists – the emotional, the relational, perhaps with the aid of a facilitator or mediator – is usually more relevant...'.

There is also a compelling argument that abuse can never be extinguished, merely *redistributed* (as one commentator once put it, 'You cannot make people moral by act of Parliament'); so one wonders whether the drive to client-protection-driven SR has more to do with a self-interested, *profession*-driven wish on the part of some practitioners to protect the 'good name' of the profession, than it has to do with reducing the net level of abuse across the helping professions as a whole. Taking the 'redistribution of abuse' theme still further, it is highly plausible that even if the more overt kinds of abuse could be effectively removed, this would merely have the effect of *institutionalising* abuse all the more subtly in the routine practices of 'professionalised therapy' itself (House, 2003) – with any such abuses being far harder, if not impossible, to spot and to legislate against. Certainly, 'Studies of disciplinary enforcement in professions in the USA have revealed that disciplinary action is extremely ineffective as a means of protecting the public' (Mowbray, 1995: 81).

There is also the danger of our irresponsibly colluding with the fantasy (or perhaps, even, unconscious *phantasy*) that it is both possible in principle, and appropriate in practice, to attempt to control and police the therapeutic process, and render it safe. Creating a comforting *illusion* of safety can, paradoxically, end up being *more* dangerous for clients than the status quo, as Richard Mowbray has convincingly argued.

The increasingly tedious refrain that, 'currently anyone can put a sign in a newsagent's window and call themselves a counsellor or psychotherapist…' is also a vacuous charge – for again, given the lack of any research evidence on whether, and if so how often, this occurs, such remarks seem little more than scare-mongering in order to generate a pretext and rationale for SR.

Finally, there exists no existing research evidence, nor any convincing logical argument, to indicate that state regulation will necessarily lessen net levels of abuse (doctors, for example, have been regulated for many years, but shocking cases still occur regularly) – yet 'the protection of clients' is still pretty much *the only* grounds invoked by pro-regulators as a rationale for state regulation.

It seems clear, then, that **there is no conceivable or demonstrable rationale for arguing that SR will reduce the net level of client/patient abuse in the psy field**; and one can therefore only conclude that the real motive behind regulation is either wholly political in nature (e.g. wishing the public to *believe* that the government is protecting them), or else is being driven by the material vested interests of professional institutions dominated by the training lobby – or, more likely, some toxic combination of the two.

Moving on from the issue of abuse, there are other concerns:

There exists substantial research from the USA demonstrating that state regulation has a number of major negative, 'general equilibrium' unintended side-effects on the field as a whole *which by far outweigh any demonstrable benefits that might stem from SR.*

A majority of practitioners work full or part time in private practice, and their work is not in any meaningful sense a branch of medicine, nor is it an activity ancillary to medicine; yet regulation through the HPC unambiguously implies, *and statutorily imposes*, non-negotiated medical values and criteria on to our work. Almost certainly a substantial majority of 'psy' practitioners do not view counselling and psychotherapy as 'medical' activities in any meaningful sense. It is therefore placing the majority of counsellors and psychotherapists into an unsustainable position of professional 'cognitive dissonance' to force the designation of 'health profession' on to their practice. Moreover, this has particularly dire consequences for an activity in which authenticity and congruence are seen as crucial characteristics of therapy practitioners' core professional identity.

Many if not most practitioners see their work as more of an art than a science – an activity that cannot be captured by a list of 'competencies' and 'standards', however elaborate; for at best, such a list can offer only a parody of actual therapeutic practice. Yet regulation by civil servants demands an 'objective' version of our practice, even if this fundamentally falsifies its nature. Any attempt to impose a quasi-objective framework of standards and competencies not only stifles creativity in the field; it also damages the therapeutic work with the client. In trying to apply a predetermined set of external principles to a particular individual, the practitioner must override the client's individuality and sacrifice the therapeutic process to the demands of a fixed technique. This is ethically unacceptable for the principled practitioner, as well as often being less than helpful therapeutically for the client.

HPC-based SR, in concert with other related, medical-model developments in the 'psy' field (Skills for Health, IAPT etc.), will tend tp reduce access to long-term, relationally oriented therapy and counselling; reduce client choice; medicalise the field; and rigidify training and inflate its cost, and hence the cost of therapy, making access to appropriate therapy help even more difficult for the economically disadvantaged and minorities.

Like many important activities, counselling and psychotherapy, though usually in some sense helpful, are inherently 'risky': they cannot be made to conform to a 'safety-first' culture, and any attempt to do so can only degrade the quality of help offered, and encourage a limited kind of 'defensive psychotherapy'. As Mowbray (1995: 150) writes, 'What is fostered by such circumstances is not a fertile and innovative field but conformity of practice based not so much on true standards... as on practitioner self-protection – the practice of "defensive psychotherapy". Practitioners will do or not do things in order to avoid disciplinary action, malpractice suits and/or the invalidating of their insurance cover, rather than solely on the basis of whether or not the client would benefit...'. HPC regulation will only reinforce existing trends towards such 'defensive practice' – that is, practice more concerned with 'playing safe' and protecting the practitioner from complaint, rather than with facilitating the client's development in the most appropriate way possible. Or put differently, clients who need therapists who have the courage and the capacity to take risks in their work will find it increasingly difficult to find them in a state-regulated psy field, thus being unable to access the healing experience that they need. At worst, we will likely end up with a programmatic kind of therapy that becomes little more than an apology for the cultural status quo.

The delicate field of therapy work is one of the last places where managerialist, 'audit culture' values and practices should hold sway. A related 'standardisation ideology' also necessarily saturates the worldview underpinning the HPC SR of the psychological therapies. The government's White Paper of several years ago, 'Trust, Assurance and Safety – The Regulation of Health Professionals in the 21st Century' (Secretary of State for Health, February 2007, Cm 7013), was shot through with the ideology of standard*isation* – and all the associated violence that such a mentality threatens to perpetrate on the rich diversity of therapy practice across the psy field. For example, on page 85, para 7.17 of the White Paper, we read the following extraordinary assertion: '…the Government believes that all professionals undertaking the same activity should be subject to the same standards of training and practice so that those who use their services can be assured that there is no difference in quality.' This single sentence grafts so many misunderstandings upon multiple misunderstandings about therapy practice that it is difficult to know where to begin. Not least, back in 1997 the Senior Policy Advisor on regulation in the Department of Health, Anne Richardson, acknowledged publicly that psychotherapy was a hugely diverse 'activity' (her term), so to refer to '*the same* activity' in this context is essentially meaningless; the phrase 'the same standards of… practice' is again to misunderstand an activity that is intrinsically unauditable and uncontrollable through the kind of 'managerialist' definitional fiat beloved of the HPC (I discuss this further, below); and finally, the very idea that it is appropriate and possible that clients be 'assured' that there is no difference in quality between practitioners' 'services' represents a wholly inappropriate intrusion of normalising consumerist values into therapy work, and ominously heralds the beginnings of the incursion of fashionable, rights-obsessed 'political correctness' into our field, where it should have no place.

SR will likely exclude from practice many part-timers and volunteers, as well as making it harder for counselling services using volunteers to survive (see below). And finally: There are clear, tried-and-tested accountability alternatives available – some of them in concrete existence in the USA and Australia – which avoid the noxious elements of current proposals; but no systematic effort seems to have been made by government to examine them.

In a world governed by any degree of rationality, the sheer force of the foregoing arguments would surely be sufficient to render any case for SR incoherent and totally unsustainable. But as suggested earlier, we live in a far from rational world, so the discussion cannot, alas, stop at this point. Rather, I now go on to comment in detail on the consultation documentation. As argued earlier, the following commentary should not be read in any way as 'suggestions for how SR might be made more palatable or acceptable', for as I have argued above, the whole project of SR is in principle fundamentally flawed in a way that no tinkering or fine-tuning can remedy.

## 3 THE HPC CONSULTATION QUESTIONS: COMMENTARY AND CRITIQUE

In this section I will only respond to those consultation questions about which I have a clear view, and I will in some cases cross-refer to other sections of this paper. Where I have no particular view or interest in the question, I have added the term 'No comment to make'.

### *Structure of the Register (section 4)*

*1. Do you agree that the Register should be structured to differentiate between psychotherapists and counsellors? If not, why not?*

> No comment to make (as to answer this question would entail that I agree with the principle of a statutory register, which I don't. See the arguments in my section 2.) In passing, however, it should be noted, first, that if there is no necessary and demonstrably consistent linear-causal relationship between length of training and competency (see my answer to question 16, below), then to use any training variable to make generalisable distinctions between (in this case) 'counselling' and 'psychotherapy' is simply non-sensical. Also, if the PLG is correct in its assertion (recommendations, p. 15) that 'differentiating between psychotherapists and counsellors would rely upon being able to identify separate standards of proficiency for each', then again, the existence of a non-linear and quite unpredictable relationship between training and competency again makes it quite impossible to make any meaningful distinction between counselling and psychotherapy.

*2. Do you agree that the Register should not differentiate between different modalities? If not, why not?*

> No comment to make (as to answer this question would entail that I agree with the principle of a statutory register, which I don't. See the arguments in my section 2.)

*3. Do you think that the Register should differentiate between practitioners qualified to work with children and young people and those qualified to work with adults? If yes, why? If not, why not?*

> No comment to make (as to answer this question would entail that I agree with the principle of a register, which I don't. See the arguments in my section 2.)

### *Protected titles (section 4.7)*

*4. Do you agree that 'psychotherapist' should become a protected title? If not, why not?*

Emphatically no. See the various arguments in my section 2, above. The very act of legally protecting this title entails the assumption that the way in which the regulator (i.e. the government, via the HPC) defines the practices of 'psychotherapy' and 'counselling' is a legitimate and widely accepted one. This is simply factually untrue: to the contrary, there is a vast literature arguing that *any* definitions of 'psychotherapy' and 'counselling' must necessarily be highly problematic, as the practice of what is called 'psychotherapy' or 'counselling' is so diverse, with so many completely incommensurable underpinning ontologies and epistemologies, that to argue for anything approaching conformable categories denoting 'psychotherapy' or 'counselling' is completely unsustainable – unless, of course, the government has decided to impose its own unavoidably partial definition upon many thousands of psy practitioners, many of whom have expressed their vehement opposition to the government's definition of what constitutes 'psychotherapy' and 'counselling'. It has also been argued that laws restricting a person's right to pursue an occupation should not be enacted unless 'The profession being regulated [has] a clearly defined field of practice adequately differentiated from other professions' (Mowbray, 1995: 90). Yet for Mowbray and many others, 'Psychotherapy is not a unified field. There is not a consensus as to the values, goals and means amongst the activities that are referred to by this label. There are instead different underlying models, with different goals and values, vying for predominance' (Mowbray, 1995: 96–7).

*See also* my section 5, below, where I comprehensively deconstruct the medical-model ideology implicit (and often explicit) in the PLG's 'Standards of Proficiency' recommendations.

5. *Do you agree that 'counsellor' should become a protected title? If not, why not?*

Emphatically no. See my answer to question 4, above.

6. *Do you agree with the approach to dual registration outlined in the report? If not, why not?*

No comment to make.

### *Voluntary register transfers (section 5)*

7. *How appropriate are the draft criteria for voluntary register transfers?*

No comment to make (as to answer this question would entail that I agree with the principle of a statutory register, which I don't. See the arguments in my section 2.)

*8. Do you have any comments on the outline process for identifying which transfers should transfer?*

No comment to make (as to answer this question would entail that I agree with the principle of a statutory register, which I don't. See the arguments in my section 2.)

*9. What evidence might an organisation holding a voluntary register provide in order to support their submission?*

No comment to make (as to answer this question would entail that I agree with the principle of a statutory register, which I don't. See the arguments in my section 2.)

***Grandparenting (section 6)***

*10. Do you agree that the grandparenting period for psychotherapists and counsellors should be set at 2 years in length?*

No comment to make (as to answer this question would entail that I agree with the principle of a statutory register, which I don't. See the arguments in my section 2.)

***Standards of proficiency (section 7)***

*11. Do you think that the standards support the recommendation to differentiate between psychotherapists and counsellors?*

No comment to make.

*12. Do you think the standards are set at the threshold level for safe and effective practice? If not, why not?*

This question is non-sensical. See my section 2. The question presupposes that it is in principle possible for such defined, normalising 'standards' first to be meaningful, and then to be translatable into the 'delivery' of 'safe and effective practice'. The picture that such a naïve ontology paints of the therapy process is completely unrecognisable to myself and, I'm sure, to thousands of psy practitioners. To claim that it is operationally possible to do this is therefore fundamentally to misrepresent the nature of the therapy experience, and therefore to perpetrate a fraud on the public.

*13. Are the draft standards applicable across modalities and applicable to work with different client groups?*

No comment to make. To answer this question would entail agreeing to the 'standards' discourse and ideology, which I strongly contest. See my section 5, below.

*14. Do you think there are any standards which should be added, amended or removed?*

See answer to previous question.

*15. Do you agree that the level of English language proficiency should be set at level 7.0 of the International English Language Testing System (IELTS) with no element below 6.5 or equivalent? (Standard 1b.3)*

No comment to make.

***Education and Training (section 8)***

*16. Do you agree that the threshold educational level for entry to the Register for counsellors should be set at level 5 on the National Qualifications Framework? If not, why not?*

No comment to make (as to answer this question would entail that I agree with the principle of a statutory register, which I don't. See the arguments in my section 2.). However, in passing it should be noted that this very question uncritically assumes that there necessarily exists some kind of positive linear-causal relationship between length of training and practitioner competence – an assumption that is not only highly problematic, but which is contradicted by a number of research studies. As (now Professor) Mark Aveline has written, '...the correlation between training and effectiveness as a therapist is low' (quoted in Mowbray, 1995: 132). This perspective also ignores the possibility of an *inverse* relationship (in some circumstances) between training and competency, in which a surfeit of 'intellectually dominated' academic training might actually *detract from* practitioners' capacity to work phenomenologically as effective therapists.

*17. Do you agree that the threshold educational level for entry to the Register for psychotherapists should be set at level 7 on the National Qualifications Framework? If not, why not?*

No comment to make (as to answer this question would entail that I agree with the principle of a statutory register, which I don't. See the arguments in my section 2.) See also answer to previous question.

***Impact assessment***

*18. Do you have any comments about the potential impact of the PLG's recommendations and the potential impact of statutory regulation?*

Yes. See my comments in section 2, above, where I present detailed arguments showing how SR, and the associated PLG recommendations, *cannot but* have negative unintended consequences on the whole psy field, with the quality, range and depth of available therapeutic help being substantially compromised, and with the net harm done to the field as a whole by SR comprehensively swamping any benefits that might conceivably flow from regulation.

***The regulation of other groups***

*19. Do you have any comments about the potential implications of this work on the future regulation of other groups delivering psychological therapies?*

If SR does pass through into law (against the will of many thousands of psy practitioners), then the very least that can be expected is that there will be *an* ***independent****, research-informed review* of the impact of regulation (and not least, on professional identities) *within three years* of SR being introduced, through which not only the appropriateness of *extending* regulation is assessed, but through which the net effects of SR are also very carefully investigated and assessed.

***Further comments***

*20. Do you have any further comments?*

Yes. See my comments throughout the rest of this paper.

## 4 THE PLG RECOMMENDATIONS: COMMENTARY AND CRITIQUE

First, it is noted that (p. 8), 'The PLG agreed that, in making its recommendations, it was important that the views of those with dissenting views or concerns about certain aspects of statutory regulation should be listened to and taken into account'. It would be instructive to know just how such 'dissenting views' as those expressed in this paper can conceivably be 'taken into account' – first because there can be no 'middle way' between the intrinsic either/or of SR or no SR; and second, because there are no members of the PLG who have known anti-regulation views. In other words, how can a group represent and take account of dissenting views when none of them agree with those views? At the risk of over-cynicism, it appears that this statement is little more than an act of lip-service appeasement which, in the brute reality of SR as it unfolds, actually has no substance whatsoever.

On p. 18, we also read that 'there is an important role post-regulation for professional bodies in continuing to shape the body of knowledge of the profession and in encouraging innovation and education'. Again, there are severe questions as to whether this can be anything more than pie-in-the-sky wishful thinking, as all the evidence from Professor Daniel B. Hogan's US research shows that innovation and creativity inevitably suffer under SR, and mainly because *the very activity* of regulation entails an intrinsic preoccupation with, and therefore bias towards, the status quo. This in-built bias towards status quo conservatism is inevitable in a regulatory system which *pre-decides* 'standards' and 'competencies' which must then be followed or met, and then statutorily enforces them; and there is simply no way round this biasing, no matter how sincere or convincing the rhetorical intentions.

As in section 3, above, the main **PLG RECOMMENDATIONS** are set out below in italic, with my comments in roman.

- *The PLG recommends that the Register should be structured to differentiate between psychotherapists and counsellors.*

  No comment to make (as to comment on this recommendation would entail that I agree with the principle of a statutory register, which I don't. See the arguments in my section 2, above.)

- *The PLG recommends that the title 'psychotherapist' should become a protected title.*

  Strongly disagree. No further comment to make (as to comment on this recommendation might entail that I agree with the principle of a statutory register, which I don't in any way. See the arguments in my section 2, above.)

- *The PLG recommends that the title 'counsellor' should become a protected title.*

  Strongly disagree. No further comment to make (as to comment on this recommendation might entail that I agree with the principle of a statutory register, which I don't in any way. See the arguments in my section 2, above.)

- *The PLG recommends the criteria for use in identifying the voluntary registers which should transfer as outlined in section 5.3, paragraph 18 of this document.*

  No comment to make (as to comment on this recommendation would entail that I agree with the principle of a statutory register, which I don't in any way. See the arguments in my section 2, above.)

- *The PLG recommends that recommendations about which voluntary registers should transfer should be made by the HPC on the basis of submissions made by organisations holding voluntary registers.*

  No comment to make (as to comment on this recommendation would entail that I agree with the principle of a statutory register, which I don't in any way. See the arguments in my section 2, above.)

- *The PLG recommends that the grandparenting period for psychotherapists and counsellors should be set at 2 years in length.*

  No comment to make (as to comment on this recommendation would entail that I agree with the principle of a statutory register, which I don't in any way. See the arguments in my section 2, above.)

- *The PLG recommends the draft standards of proficiency outlined in appendix 2 of this document for consultation.*

  I offer detailed comments on these proposals below in section 5, with the strong proviso that this does not in any way imply that I believe that tinkering with these draft standards would in any way render SR more palatable, for as made clear earlier, in my view this is in principle impossible.

- *The PLG recommends that the 'normal' threshold level of qualification for entry to the Register should be set as follows:*

  *- For counsellors, level 5 on the National Qualifications Framework / Intermediate level on the Framework for Higher Education Qualifications / level 8/9 on the Scottish Credit and Qualifications Framework.*

  *- For psychotherapists, level 7 on the National Qualifications Framework / M level on the Framework for Higher Education Qualifications / level 11 on the Scottish Credit and Qualifications Framework.*

  See my answers to questions 1 and 16 in section 3, above. In sum, as there is no demonstrable linear-causal relationship between competency and length or type of training, it is non-sensical, and has no evidence base, to make such a hierarchical distinction between counselling and psychotherapy.

## 5 'STANDARDS OF PROFICIENCY': COMMENTARY AND CRITIQUE

On page 1 of the HPC consultation document, we read that 'To protect the public, we [the HPC] set standards that professionals must meet'; and 'the HPC must publish standards for each of the regulated professions which are the "necessary" or "threshold" considered to be essential for safe and effective practice' (PLG recommendations, p. 35). And on p. 29 of the PLG recommendations, we read that 'The voluntary register must demonstrate processes for assuring that applicants meet the required standards of entry…', with the term 'the standards of proficiency for the profession' being used on p. 32, and the term 'generic standards' on p. 36. Many other such tell-tale examples could be given, of course – one of the worst being the extraordinary embracing of 'audit speak' by the PLG itself, when it refers to '*delivering* standards' on p. 40 (para 12, my italics). (Incidentally, in the copy of the PLG document that I have, I counted no less than *nearly 30* instances of the term 'deliver/delivered/delivering' etc.).

It is clear, therefore, that the HPC and the PLG believe that counselling and psychotherapy constitute activities for which it is possible *in principle,* and appropriate *in practice,* to define universalising generic standards, that can be generalised across the psy field. In what follows I will argue that this latter is a fundamental misunderstanding of the unique and subtle nature of therapy practice, uncritically embracing, as it does, a late-modernist paradigm (including the anxiety-driven surveillance and audit cultures) just at the time when, culturally and historically, the paradigm of 'modernity' is under sustained philosophical, political and spiritual challenge in a whole host of ways. I believe that the psy therapies should be at the forefront of these paradigmatic challenges, and should certainly not be colluding with and reinforcing a moribund paradigm of late modernity in its death throes; for SR will inevitably have such a pernicious effect.

It would be all too easy (but tedious) to trawl through the minutiae of the PLG's draft 'Standards of proficiency for psychotherapists and counsellors', for doing this would be to sanction the view that it is in principle both possible and appropriate to specify such standards in a programmatic way in the psy field – a view which I unreservedly reject. It is at this point in this paper where the issue of *incommensurable paradigms* (in the Kuhnian sense) becomes most acute; for from a 'new paradigm', transpersonal or trans- or critical postmodern perspective – which privileges, for example, the unknown, *un*learning, 'negative capability' (Keats) and practising 'without memory or desire' (Bion) – the specification of standards and competencies 'before the event' is fundamentally to misunderstand and to misspecify that which is central in the practice of many therapists in their work (several thousands of whom have already signed petitions against these wrong-headed proposals).

Within education – a field in which I have been particularly engaged with these issues – Lynn Fendler,[1] for example, has developed the kind of critique of the standards-obsessed positivistic discourse that has been notably missing in any deliberations about the appropriateness of state-regulating psy activity via a standards-based ideology. Below, I reproduce an aspect of her incisive critique, substituting 'therapy' for 'education' terms (as precisely the same arguments apply in both fields):

> 'Now there is a reversal; the goals and outcomes are being stipulated at the outset, and the procedures are being developed post hoc. The "nature" of the [client's experience] is stipulated in advance, based on

> objective criteria, usually statistical analysis. Because the outcome drives the procedure (rather than vice versa), there is no longer the theoretical possibility of unexpected results; there is no longer the theoretical possibility of becoming unique in the process of becoming ['treated']... In this new system, evaluation of [psychotherapeutic] policy reform is limited to an evaluation of the degree to which any given procedure yields the predetermined results...'

Similarly, Professor Andrew Cooper[2] has been one of the few therapist commentators directly to engage with the pernicious effects of the 'audit culture'. In his seminal 2001 paper, he writes:

> 'We now live in a relentlessly superintended world, a quangoed regime of commissioners, inspectors, and regulators... [quoting Peter Preston], [and] important questions of truth, meaning and authenticity are sacrificed on the altar of compulsive reassurance of the critical superintendent... Fundamental principles about freedom, autonomy and citizenship are threatened by this state of affairs... Obsessional activity... is essentially about control rather than creativity... These systems may be contributing to a deterioration of standards, while maintaining a pretence that they are achieving the opposite.' (Cooper, 2001: *passim*)

There surely exist very considerable dangers indeed in the therapy world engaging with this pernicious *Zeitgeist* – one which is arguably quite antithetical to the core values of therapeutic work at its best, and of which standards-driven state regulation can be seen to be the crowning 'glory'. Moreover, and as argued earlier, one of the many strong arguments against state regulation is that it will have the effect of cementing in place a (self-interested and self-reinforcing) 'profession' in a way that unavoidably privileges the status quo – and this for an activity at the centre of which, for many of us, lie the core irreducible values of flexibility, creativity, freedom and therapy as *a culturally evolving healing practice*. On this view, it is especially ironic that the PLG recommendations propose that registrants 'understand the role of the therapist in the broader social and cultural context' (p. 4). From the perspective of this paper, if registrants were to genuinely and deeply engage with such an understanding, they would immediately resign from colluding in a process that can only place a fetter on the healthy evolution of therapy work in late-modern culture.

One reason why therapy has arguably been such an effective and successful cultural practice over many decades is *precisely because* there has not (yet) been any concerted attempt to control, 'can', and colonise 'therapy' in relation to any external or 'statist' agenda; and it is inevitable that the fundamental nature of psy activity will be changed by these wrong-headed SR proposals, and in directions that cannot but compromise precisely those conditions that have made therapy so successful. As argued earlier, this view is also entirely consistent with the Steinerian conception of the Threefold Social Order (lying, crucially, beyond both socialism and capitalism),[3] in which it is seen as essential that the activity of the cultural sphere in society is left relatively free from, and unhindered by, either political (politicised) or financial/economic interests.

Now, briefly, to the draft standards themselves. As already mentioned, they are shot through with medical-model terminology and assumptions, the existence of which is certainly not some unfortunate oversight by the PLG group, but which is, rather, a direct and inevitable consequence of the worldview that they unavoidably embrace in engaging in the discourse of 'generic standards', 'competencies' and regulation more generally. Presumably the PLG started out as it meant to go along! – i.e. 'Registrant psychotherapists *must*...' (my italics). Extraordinary. One wonders whether the people making up this group have ever read anything by (e.g.) Winnicott about compliance, and its shadow. The PLG recommendations also contain tell-tale language that consistently betrays the worldview and its quasi-authoritarian dynamics that underpin this document: for example, 'what is *required of them* by the HPC'; '*manage* the dynamics of power' '*must* be able to justify their decisions', and so on (all italics added).

The draft guidelines go on, first, to speak (disingenuously?) about professional *autonomy* (and accountability), and the 'autonomous professional'. Again, extraordinary. There seems no appreciation here that, first, the very act of statutorily imposed regulation cannot but encroach into any so-called practitioner 'autonomy'; and second, that practitioner autonomy is just assumed, over and above (for example) co-created client–therapist Levinasian *hetero*nomy; and there seems to be no awareness of the naïvely humanistic ontology which is being assumed here, and the therapist-centred discourse to which it gives rise.

I have already referred on several occasions to the medical-model worldview that must inevitably underpin a 'profession' that is about to regulated by the *Health* Professions Council. Thus, on p. 4 of the recommendations we read that 'service users' need to be engaged in 'evaluating diagnostics, treatments and interventions to meet their needs and goals'. As the psychiatrist famously said in a memorable *Fawlty Towers* episode, 'there's enough material there for a whole conference!'. For example, is the PLG aware of the devastating critiques coming out of the critical psychiatry field (e.g. see Mary Boyle's and Ian Parker's work) on the ideology of the 'diagnostic' mentality?; does the PLG group really want to speak in terms of 'treatments'?; is meeting the (presumably conscious) needs and 'goals' of clients always the appropriate therapeutic stance to take in therapy work? What on earth is any registrant supposed to do if they fundamentally disagree with the whole tenor and discourse of this document? To what degree of professional incongruence, dissonance or identity distortion do they have to subject themselves, in order to 'shoe-horn' themselves into these recommendations?

More medical-model, 'managerialist' terminology and practices are uncritically embraced throughout the document. Thus, under 'Identification and assessment of health and social care needs' (pp. 6–9), we read of 'assessment techniques'; 'problem-solving (skills)'; 'intervention plans'; 'be[ing] able to engage in evidence-based practice' and 'outcome measures' (thereby assuming that actual/phenomenological therapy experience/practice is amenable to nomothetic research findings, which many anti-positivistic practitioners and authorities completely refute); 'be able to audit… practice' and 'audit trails'; 'quality assurance'; 'management plans'; 'techniques'; 'procedures'; and 'working towards continual improvement' (i.e. the 'driving-up standards' ideology of the audit culture). And under 'Knowledge, understanding and skills' (pp. 10–11), 'knowledge of… disorder and dysfunction'; 'scientific inquiry' (presumably meaning positivist science); 'treatment efficacy'; 'psychopathology'; 'mental disorder'; 'conduct appropriate diagnostic procedures' (cf. earlier); and 'treatment methods'. At the risk of over-labouring the point, it's just not good enough for the PLG to argue that (for example) 'this is just our way of expressing commonly/universally held views about therapy theory and practice, and we could simply use different language'. The fact is that this deliberately chosen discourse denotes a worldview that is deeply alien to a very considerable number of psy practitioners, and it is *intrinsic* to regulatory ideology; and (hopefully), these characteristics might well ultimately qualify this document as one of the longest suicide notes in regulatory history.

Moreover, the advocacy of 'a coherent framework of psychological theory and evidence' (p. 7) again presupposes that such a theory-driven worldview is appropriate to therapy practice, which for many practitioners, and certainly those of a postmodern, phenomenological-existential and transpersonal orientation, it simply isn't. And again, because these are presented as *statutory requirements* for all registrants, then it is very difficult to see how a substantial number of existing practitioners will be able to agree to such alien impositions on their work. As Mowbray puts it, 'Whilst the acquisition of an elaborate body of professional knowledge may be fundamental to competence in the typical profession, there is little reason to suppose that basic competence in psychotherapy… is founded on a similar basis' (1995: 12). For Mowbray, 'Some of the best practitioners may *not* be applying a "developed body of psychological theory"' in their work (ibid.: 123).

I will end these disparate critical comments on the draft PLG 'Standards of Proficiency' recommendation to reiterate the point that **any tinkering with**

**the wording or the substance of these recommendations cannot in any way make acceptable and appropriate the goal (i.e. state regulation), in the service of which agenda they have been fashioned.** Moreover, the series of incongruent and incoherent recommendations in this document are not some aberration or rectifiable 'mistake', but rather are symptomatic of the flawed quarry of state regulation, and the regulatory mind-set and accompanying ideology into which PLG members have had to insert themselves, quite possibly dramatically distorting their own professional mores and identities in the process, in order to 'deliver' what they have been charged to 'deliver' (in this document, at least 29 times....).

A number of other points from the PLG recommendations document deserve brief mention. First, regarding the issue of **diversity**, on p. 36 the PLG writes that 'During its substantial deliberations on the standards, the PLG discussed the diversity of practice across psychotherapy and counselling and the diversity of education and training'. And?... – errr, that's it?.... As if by just asserting that such a discussion was had will somehow magically mean that the core principles of diversity and pluralism are enshrined in the 'proficiency standards'! From the perspective offered in this paper, this should have been *just the start* of the discussion – i.e. how can the desire for and specification of generalised generic standards be compatible with the core values of diversity and pluralism in psy practice? It is symptomatic of the lack of understanding of these complexities and dangers within the PLG group that they essentially ignore them. Or a different interpretation: this ignoring is hardly surprising, for to even begin to engage in this discussion would very soon expose the whole regulatory process for the incoherent impossibility that it is.

Next, in terms of 'Scope of practice' (p. 36), we read that 'As long as [registrants] *make sure* that they are practising safely and effectively within their given scope of practice *and do not practise in the areas in which they are not proficient to do so*, this is not problematic' (italics added). This statement again betrays the paradigmatic chasm that exists between those who are responsible for this mooted regulatory process, and a major proportion of therapists who will simply reject out of hand the assumptions and associated world-view on which the latter statement is based. As if it is within anyone's conscious control that safe practice can be *ensured* in psy work; or, as if it is either possible or appropriate to somehow be programmatically prepared to work with certain kinds of clients/patients and/or presenting issues (which of course will all be transparent from the outset!), and not with others.

We also read that 'The voluntary register must demonstrate evidence that members are expected to demonstrate a commitment to CPD' (p. 29). The area of Continuing Professional Development is a very complex question, with which complexities the PLG makes no attempt to engage. To give just one example: from a critical postmodern perspective, the very creation of a category called 'CPD' has the effect of 'thingifying' the process of practitioner development, and somehow assuming in a 'low-trust', infantilising way that practitioners simply can't be trusted to pursue their own development in their own way, without being subject to compulsory injunctions by the goverment. No attempt is made by the PLG to engage with these kinds of legitimate critiques; rather, CPD and its imposition are assumed to be an unproblematic given. We can surely expect far higher 'standards' of critical thinking in this of all fields; yet critical, independent thinking is, again, one of the first casualties of any mind-set that expediently embraces the principle of generic standardisation and the alleged but chimerical virtues of state regulation of a field as diverse as ours.

There are also major problems with any attempt to 'academicise' the activities of psychotherapy and counselling. It has been argued by a number of commentators (including Professor Ian Parker and myself) that the Academy is by no means the most appropriate location for therapy training to be located, not least because the qualities that make for effective practitionership are not only not exclusively academic in nature, but the preoccupation with theory and 'the rational-academic' which dominates the Academy can be argued to be antithetical to effective practitionership. On this view, such universal academicisation of trainings cannot but reduce the diversity of practitioners in the field as a whole. Thus, it can therefore be argued that the proposal that (for example) level 7 on the NQF be the level for psychotherapists to enter the register is entirely inappropriate, and cannot but narrow the field as a whole (level 7 is defined, of course, as 'postgraduate certificates, postgraduate diplomas and masters degrees or equivalent' – p. 44, para 36). According to Mowbray, 'There is little if any evidence that the possession of academic qualifications by psychotherapists relates to basic competence or protects the public in any way.... [I]ncreasing the academic prerequisites and content do not favour the most important variables that relate to basic competence in this area.... The personal qualities that are prerequisites of competence in this sort of activity cannot be "trained in"....' (Mowbray, 1995: 116, 118). Moreover, and perhaps counterintuitively, 'there is no clear evidence that professionally trained psychotherapists are in general more effective than paraprofessionals' (ibid.: 116).

Next, the highly complex notion of 'informed consent' is merely uncritically asserted (e.g. pp. 2 and 5), rather than engaged with and argued through. Again, this is by no means a mere oversight: rather, from the late-modernist mindset of 'standards' and 'competencies', of course the PLG *has* to claim that 'informed consent' is both possible and unproblematic; for to admit that it isn't, and in principle never can be in therapy work, would again fundamentally undermine any attempt it makes procedurally to specify, and 'make safe' from the outset, what is an always unfolding and inherently unpredictable therapeutic experience.

A final point. It seems extraordinary that **the grandparenting route** to the mooted register will cost an applicant £420 (see p. 33, para 14). Let us be clear: it will often be the case that those needing to be 'grandparented' will be long-standing voluntary counsellors who have either worked for voluntary agencies for many years, or who work (very) part-time, and who have vast practical experience. The very idea that it should cost these stalwart counsellors over £400 to sign up to a register, for which there exists no evidence base that it will raise genuine standards in the psy field as a whole, or enhance public protection, is nothing short of outrageous. More generally, this seems yet another graphic example of the way in which government-driven SR is going to have substantial cost implications for a crucial and invaluable sector of the psy field – and it will inevitably have the effect of both reducing the supply of therapeutic help to society, and creating severe financial difficulties for many voluntary agencies. Again, finally, it must be emphasised that to make any concessions on this point has no implications whatsoever regarding the advisability of SR as a principle, which is comprehensively contra-indicated by all the evidence in this submission.

**Section notes:**

1 L. Fendler, 'What is it impossible to think? A genealogy of the educated subject', in T.S. Popkewitz and M. Brennan (eds), *Foucault's Challenge: Discourse, Knowledge and Power in Education*, Teachers College Press, Columbia University, New York, 1998, p. 57.

2 A. Cooper, 'The state of mind we're in: social anxiety, governance and the audit society', *Psychoanalytic Studies*, 3 (3-4), 2001, pp. 349-62 (quotation, *passim*).

3 See, for example, M. Large, *Common Wealth*, Hawthorn Press, Stroud, 2010 (in press), and R. Steiner, *The Threefold Social Order*, New Economy Publications, 1996.

## 6 COMMENTARY

It would be a major error of judgement for the government to underestimate the extent of opposition to these ill-thought-through proposals, and the focused resolve of a substantial proportion of the psy field to oppose them in every possible way. It has been a commonly held view for several decades – including, till recently, amongst the government's own Senior Policy Advisors – that it would be quite impossible to regulate a field whose inherent diversity and pluralism by far exceeds any meaningful coherence in terms of theoretical base and principled approaches to therapy practice. The dramatic eruption of practitioner dissent of recent months, not least through the Alliance for Counselling and Psychotherapy of which I am a proud and active member, merely confirms the wisdom of that earlier view.

A major research consultation is clearly called for, in which existing research on the general-equilibrium effects of regulation are collated and carefully considered, and in which actual practitioners are extensively consulted (as distinct from the professional groupings that notionally 'represent' them, with their associated profession-centred and training interests). *The government should immediately announce a delay to the process of HPC regulation, while the whole issue is subject to such a wide-ranging enquiry by an independent commission*, whose remit will be to investigate whether existing accountability frameworks are adequate, or can be suitably enhanced, without the need for HPC or additional state regulation. As the organisation which represents by far the widest range of therapeutic modalities in the history of the field, the Alliance for Counselling and Psychotherapy should also be involved in any DoH consultation process on accountability and regulation, as the Alliance represents a rapidly growing body of opinion that is beyond any institutional vested interest – unlike the other major institutional players in the psy field.

With regard to the issue of abuse in the psy field, one can only wonder why it is, if this is such an urgent issue requiring state regulation, that the HPC and the Department of Health have not carried out their own up-to-date empirical research on the extent of 'the abuse problem' in Britain. Why, we may well ask, after over a century of psy activity unregulated by the state, is the field now being exposed to potentially devastating changes, when abuse and unethical practice in the past was almost certainly far more widespread than it is today, and when the research base to support those changes is entirely lacking? Moreover, has there been any attempt by pro-regulators psycho-socially to locate these changes in the wider cultural trends captured by terms like 'the age of anxiety', 'the risk-averse society' and 'the low-trust society'? Is SR far more a case of 'pathological' acting-out than it is a case of mature and considered response to real concerns? Many of us believe that it is.

There are also all manner of possible accountability procedures that *already exist* in the psy field, and alongside which, new innovative procedures could be built. The latter would likely be far more effective than the HPC regulation route in responding to abuse (e.g. greatly enhanced public education about therapy; the favouring of mediation and 'working-through' over legalistic 'blame and shame' procedures, and so on) – but without any of the deleterious unintended side-effects on the field that Daniel B. Hogan's research strongly suggests will inevitably stem from HPC regulation. It has been argued that laws restricting a person's right to pursue an occupation should not be enacted unless 'Simpler and less restrictive methods that would accomplish the same purposes [are] unavailable (for example existing laws)' (Mowbray, 1995: 90). Yet (Mowbray again), 'The existing situation regarding psychotherapy does not in general warrant any legislative changes other than what can usefully be effected as part of a general improvement in consumer legislation by legislative encouragement of the truthful, full disclosure of information relevant to any service, product or undertaking being offered for a reward. Such a general improvement in consumer legislation... would provide a cost-effective way of improving the existing situation regarding psychotherapy without the negative side-effects of creating a statutory monopoly.... Laws that are applicable in this area as elsewhere include those concerning contracts, deception, truth in advertising (trade description), assault and breach of confidence' (Mowbray, 1995: 215–16, 205).

It is therefore grossly irresponsible – and it amounts to playing Russian Roulette with the future well-being of the psy field – to be pursuing what, for many, is an alien regulatory path, before all such possible remedies under existing structures have been investigated. That this has clearly not occurred strongly reinforces the suspicion of many of us that the willing compliance with HPC regulation by certain key, powerful individuals within the psy field has far more to do with vested interest and the ultra-competitive positioning of the training organisations than it has to do with any authentic concern for client/patient well-being.

As argued earlier in this paper, even if regulation *were* to succeed in 'weeding out' a few 'rogue' practitioners, all the research evidence shows that any such benefits will be swamped by the negative unintended consequences for the field – and again, the pro-regulators have never even attempted to respond to the compelling research evidence about negative unintended side-effects of SR, despite being repeatedly challenged in print and in public to do so. Such deafening silence again strongly suggests that the drive for regulation has far more to do with vested interests and blatant empire-building than it has to do with the oft-mooted but threadbare rationale of 'protection of the public' (see section 2, above).

There is also the key question of practitioner competence. If it is so that '...the effectiveness of psychotherapy does not appear to depend upon any of the following: (1) The practitioner holding academic qualifications; (2) The length of training of the practitioner; (3) The school to which the therapist belongs; and (4) The practitioner having had a training analysis' (Mowbray, 1995: 122), then severe doubt must be cast upon any regulatory system which claims that competence *can* somehow be guaranteed by such an approach and the associated 'competency criteria'. *At worst, a misleading fraud is being perpetrated upon the public to pretend that effectiveness in the practice of counselling and psychotherapy can be legislated into existence in this way*. Moreover, '...[E]stablishing entry requirements [to the profession] that are not highly correlated with effectiveness restricts the size of the pool of people from whom the prospective client can choose an appropriate practitioner for themselves... [In choosing a practitioner to work with] there are no easily applied external qualifications that you can trust' (ibid.: 124, 127).

## 7 CONCLUSIONS: PRESERVING A 'COUNTERCULTURAL SPACE'

Historically, counselling and psychotherapy have been conducted in a private, confidential space, free of externally defined, institutionally driven agendas, in which clients can take matters of deep personal concern for dialogical exploration and reflection. The therapeutic space is one of late-modern society's last surviving bastions against, and refuges from, narrowly stultifying mechanistic thinking, and from the intrusive compliance experiences that bring many, if not most, clients into therapy in the first place.

State regulation constitutes a gross intrusion into this culturally unique private space, and the government's control-fixated agenda can only compromise the quality of that space. There is, therefore, an urgent need to protect the consulting room from this unwarranted government colonisation; and these non-evidence-based developments can only fuel suspicions that regulation of the 'psy' field is merely the latest symptom of a wider cultural movement towards a 'surveillance society', in which, not least, therapy becomes inappropriately annexed to a governmental social-engineering agenda. Thus, for Mowbray, the non-medical model 'human potential' work that he advocates, and which he vigorously distinguishes from medical-model 'psychotherapy', is a practice that 'must stay on the margin and not be "absorbed", not be tempted by the carrots of recognition, respectability and financial security into reverting to the mainstream but rather remain – on the "fringe" – as a source that stimulates, challenges convention and "draws out" the unrealized potential for "being" in the members of that society' (Mowbray, 1995: 198–9). Moreover,

> 'A society needs a healthy fringe – a fringe that is on the edge but not split-off in cult-like isolation. It is the seedbed from which much of what is novel will spring. It is where ideas that are ahead of their time will germinate and grow, later to be adopted by the mainstream. In order to remain a fertile seedbed, the fringe needs to be legitimate rather than driven underground or "criminalized" – which would stifle it, but also it must not be absorbed into the mainstream – which would stultify it with "establishment" thinking and respectability... the

possibility of… statutory endorsement poses a threat to the vitality of the "fringe"' (ibid.: 199, 200).

A significant number of therapists – undoubtedly running into thousands – are implacably opposed to regulation of the psychological therapies via the HPC, and will simply refuse to comply with it, via the emerging therapeutic ethic of '**Principled Non-Compliance**'.

A final point can perhaps be made in terms of the well-known 'precautionary principle'. At the very least, the multiple arguments in both this paper, and in other critical submissions to the HPC emanating from the Alliance for Counselling and Psychotherapy, point to the need for a strict *precautionary principle* to be applied in this area, when the alleged benefits of SR are merely being anecdotally asserted, and no attempt has been made by government to research into either the advisability or the cost/benefit balance to the psy field as a whole of implementing SR. *All the available evidence points to the conclusion that any benefits that might stem from state regulation will be swamped by the negative unintended side-effects*. And any refusal of government to launch the kind of independent inquiry advocated above will merely prove to any dispassionate observer that the non-evidence-based drive towards to SR has nothing whatsoever to do with rational argumentation, or 'protection of the public', and everything to do with (some toxic combination of) expedient politicisation, 'caught-up-ness' in the ideological late-modernist paradigm in its death throes, or powerful training vested interests and power-driven empire-building. Those of us who care deeply about the future of psy work will do everything within our influence to ensure that these alien values do not prevail.

## APPENDIX

### Publications on psychotherapy Regulation and Professionalisation by Richard House

(1) 'Peer accreditation... within a humanistic framework?', *Self and Society: European Journal of Humanistic Psychology*, 19 (2), 1991, pp. 33-6 (co-author: Jill Hall)

(2) '"Audit-mindedness" in counselling: some underlying dynamics', *British Journal of Guidance and Counselling*, 24 (2), 1996, pp. 277-83; also in *Implausible Professions* (ed. House and Totton), PCCS Books, 1997, pp. 63-70

(3) 'The dynamics of professionalisation: a personal view on counselling research', *Counselling* (BAC), 8 (3), 1997, pp. 200-4; also in *Implausible Professions* (ed. House and Totton), PCCS Books, 1997, pp. 51-62

(4) Letter on the Independent Therapists' Network, *Self and Society*, 23 (3), 1995, p. 46

(5) Review of Richard Mowbray's Case against Psychotherapy Registration (Trans Marginal Press, London, 1995), *Changes: International Journal of Psychology and Psychotherapy*, 14 (1), 1996, pp. 85-7

(6) *Mowbray Distilled: A Summary of his* The Case Against Psychotherapy Registration, 16-page pamphlet produced by the Independent Practitioners Network and widely circulated within the field and beyond; *available on request;* reprinted with a new introduction in *Ipnosis* magazine, 13 and 14, 2004 (pp. 4-7 and 27-9)

(7) 'The professionalisation of counselling: a coherent 'case against'? *Counselling Psychology Quarterly*, 9 (4), 1996, pp. 343-58

(8) Review of Richard Mowbray's *Case Against Psychotherapy Registration* (Trans Marginal Press, London), *Clinical Psychology Forum*, December 1995, pp. 43-4

(9) Letter on professionalisation, *Self and Society*, 23 (5), 1995, p. 49

(10) *Implausible Professions: Arguments for Pluralism and Autonomy in Psychotherapy and Counselling* (co-editor, Nick Totton), PCCS Books, Ross-on-Wye, 1997

(11) 'The dynamics of power', *Counselling News*, 20 (Dec.), 1995, pp. 24-5

(12) 'Registration is dead?... Mowbray's case against bureaucratic professionalisation', mimeo, privately circulated

(13) 'Letter to Stephen Dorrell MP' (re the Department of Health's attitude to statutory registration), reproduced in *PiN: Newsletter for the Independent Practitioners Network*, 5, 1996, pp. 9-10

(14) 'Letter' (response to Digby Tantam on professionalisation), *Self and Society*, 24 (3), 1996, pp. 54-5

(15 Professional vs. vocational training in counsellor development', 1996, mimeo, privately circulated

(16 'The registration debate: an illusion of policing', *Human Potential*, Winter 1996/7, p. 13

(17 'Introduction' (with N. Totton), in *Implausible Professions* (ed. House and Totton), PCCS Books, 1997, pp. 1-10

(18) 'Conclusion' (with N. Totton), in *Implausible Professions* (ed. House and Totton), PCCS Books, 1997, pp. 335-7

(19) 'Training: a guarantee of competence?, in *Implausible Professions* (ed. House and Totton), PCCS Books, 1997, pp. 99-108

(20) 'Therapy in New Paradigm perspective: the phenomenon of Georg Groddeck', in *Implausible Professions* (ed. House and Totton), PCCS Books, 1997, pp. 225-40

(21) 'Participatory ethics in a self-generating practitioner community', in *Implausible Professions* (ed. House and Totton), PCCS Books, 1997, pp. 323-34

(22) 'Correspondence: Registering concern about professionalisation', *British Journal of Guidance and Counselling*, 25 (1), 1997, pp. 107-10

(23) 'From professionalisation towards a post-therapy era', *Self and Society*, 25 (2), 1997, pp. 31-5

(24) 'A professionalised fetish can be made of supervision' (anonymously published), *The Therapist*, 4 (4), 1997, p. 23

(25) Review of I. James and S. Palmer (eds), *Professional Therapeutic Titles: Myths and*

*Realities* (BPS, Div. Couns. Psychol. Occ. Paper, 1996), *British Journal of Guidance and Counselling,* 26 (1), 1998, pp. 128-9

(26) 'Rival registers?' (Letter to the editor), *Counselling,* 9 (1), 1998, p. 3

(27) ' "Limits to counselling and therapy": deconstructing a professional ideology', *British Journal of Guidance and Counselling,* 27 (3), 1999, pp. 377-92; reprinted in *Ethically Challenged Professions: Enabling Innovation and Diversity in Psychotherapy and Counselling,* (ed. Bates and House), PCCS Books, 2003, pp. 94-109

(28) Letter to the Editor (on Michael Pokorny's response to Postle 1998), *International Journal of Psychotherapy,* 4 (2), 1999, pp. 263-4

(29) 'The place of psychotherapy and counselling in a healthy European social order: a commentary on Tantam and van Deurzen', *European Journal of Psychotherapy, Counselling and Health,* 2 (2), 1999, pp. 237-44

(30) 'Deconstruction, post-?-modernism and the future of psychotherapy' (review feature on Ian Parker [ed.], *Deconstructing Psychotherapy,* Sage, 1999), *The Psychotherapy Review,* 1 (7), 1999, pp. 322-32

(31) Letter to the Editor (on the future of therapy), *Self and Society,* 28 (1), 2000, p. 59

(32) 'Psychotherapy professionalization: the post-graduate dimension and the legitimacy of statutory regulation', *British Journal of Psychotherapy,* 17 (3), 2001, pp. 382-90; reprinted in two parts *Ipnosis: An Independent Journal for Practitioners,* 5 (Spring), 2002, pp. 28-9; and 7 (Autumn, 2002), pp. 26-7

(33) 'The statutory regulation of psychotherapy: still time to think again', *The Psychotherapist,* 17, 2001, pp. 12-17; reprinted in *Ethically Challenged Professions: Enabling Innovation and Diversity in Psychotherapy and Counselling,* (ed. Bates and House), PCCS Books, 2003, pp. 142-7; see website http://www.uea.ac.uk/~wp276/article.htm

(34) Unpublished Letter to the Editor on regulation, submitted to *Counselling and Psychotherapy Journal,* published in *Ipnosis: An Independent Journal for Practitioners,* 3 (Autumn), 2001, p. 15

(35) 'A response to Frans Loman' (to his 'What is so bad with academicization of training?'), *Newsletter of the Universities Psychotherapy and Counselling Association,* 7 (Autumn), 2001, pp. 12-13

(36) *Therapy Beyond Modernity: Deconstructing and Transcending Profession-Centred Therapy,* Karnac Books, London, 2003

(37) 'Ahead of his time: Carl Rogers on "professionalism", 1973', *Ipnosis: An Independent Journal for Practitioners,* 6 (Summer), 2002, pp. 20-2

(38) 'Reflections and elaborations on "post-professionalized" therapy practice – book excerpt', *Ipnosis: An Independent Journal for Practitioners,* 8 (Winter), 2002, reprinted in *Ethically Challenged Professions: Enabling Innovation and Diversity in Psychotherapy and Counselling,* (ed. Bates and House), PCCS Books, 2003, pp. 247-56

(39) *Ethically Challenged Professions: Enabling Innovation and Diversity in Psychotherapy and Counselling* (co-editor, Yvonne Bates), PCCS Books, Ross-on-Wye, 2003

(40) 'Introduction' and 'Conclusion' (with Yvonne Bates), in *Ethically Challenged Professions: Enabling Innovation and Diversity in Psychotherapy and Counselling,* (ed. Bates and House), PCCS Books, 2003, pp. iii-iv and 298-300

(41) 'Therapy beyond modernity' (book extract), *Ipnosis: An Independent Journal for Practitioners*, 8 (Winter), 2002, pp. 14-18

(42) 'An unqualified good: The IPN as a path through and beyond professionalisation', *Self and Society*, 32 (4), 2004, pp. 14-22

(43) *Mowbray Distilled: A Summary of his* The Case Against Psychotherapy Registration, with a new introduction, *Ipnosis* magazine, 13 and 14, 2004 (pp. 4-7 and 27-9, respectively)

(44) 'Commentary: difference, the "profession", and transcending the ideologies of late modernity: a response to Oakley', *European Journal of Psychotherapy, Counselling and Health*, 6 (4), 2003, pp. 281-92; see website http://www.uea.ac.uk/~wp276/article.htm

(45) 'Healing beyond modernity and professionalisation? A review article', *Ipnosis* magazine, 18 (Summer), 2005, pp. 28-30

(46) 'The state regulation of counselling and psychotherapy: sometime, never…?', *Journal of Critical Psychology, Counselling and Psychotherapy*, 5 (4), 2005, pp.176-89; available at:

http://ipnosis.postle.net/pages/RHouseRegulationSometimeNever.htm

(47) 'Interview', published in the online journal, *Europe's Journal of Psychology* – psy.journal@gmail.com, November 2005

(48) 'The be-coming of a therapist: experiential learning, self-education and the personal/professional nexus', *British Journal of Guidance and Counselling*, 35 (4), 2007, pp. 427-40

(49) 'For PNC and ATP - comments on the Psychotherapy and Counselling Reference Group Meeting, 29 March 2007', *Ipnosis* magazine, 26 (Summer), 2007, pp. 28-9

(50) 'Unconsciously generating inevitability? Workable accountability alternatives to the statutory regulation of the psychological therapies' (co-author, Denis Postle), in I. Parker and S. Revelli (eds), *Psychoanalytic Practice and State Regulation*, Karnac Books, London, 2008, pp. 191-203

(51) 'Training and education for therapy practitionership: "trans-modern" perspectives', *Counselling Psychology Quarterly*, 21 (1), 2008, pp. 1-10

(52) 'The dance of psychotherapy and politics', *Psychotherapy and Politics International*, 6 (2), 2008, pp. 98-109

(53) 'Therapy's modernist "regime of truth": from scientistic "theory-mindedness" towards the subtle and the mysterious', *Philosophical Practice*, 3 (3), 2008, pp. 343-52

(54) 'Towards post-professional practice: principled non-compliant practitionership in a post-regulation era', *Self and Society*, 36 (2), 2008, pp. 44-50

(55) 'Empirically supported/validated treatments as modernist ideology: I: Dodo, manualization, and the paradigm question' (co-author Arthur C. Bohart), in

R. House and D. Loewenthal (eds), *Against and For CBT: Towards a Constructive Dialogue?* PCCS Books, Ross-on-Wye, 2008, pp. 188-201

(56) 'Empirically supported/validated treatments as modernist ideology: II: Alternative perspectives on research and practice' (co-author Arthur C. Bohart), in R. House and D. Loewenthal (eds), *Against and For CBT: Towards a Constructive Dialogue?* PCCS Books, Ross-on-Wye, 2008, pp. 202-17

(57) 'On the inadvisability of state regulating the psychological therapies: Submission to the HPC's 'Call for ideas', *Ipnosis* magazine, 34, 2009, in press

(58) 'Still Time to Stop the Regulatory Juggernaut: The new Alliance for Counselling and Psychotherapy against State Regulation – arguments and resources', *Ipnosis* magazine, 34, 2009, in press

## Other Supporting Literature and Resources

**eIpnosis – http://ipnosis.org: a** website packed with information and opinion undermining the basis for HPC regulation.

**College of Psychoanalysts website News Pages** at:

http://www.psychoanalysis-cpuk.org/latest%20news.html

**The Psychoanalytic Consortium website** at:

http://psychoanalyticconsortium.org/

***The Regulation of Psychotherapists*** (4 volumes) – by Daniel B. Hogan (Ballinger, New York, 1979) – a classic, four-volume analysis of research and experience which comes down firmly against HPC-style regulation. Never refuted, little discussed by the supporters of statutory/state regulation.

***The Case Against Psychotherapy Regulation*** – by Richard Mowbray (Trans Marginal Press, London, 1995) – a prophetic book from a growth movement perspective, which also gives a thorough summary of Hogan's work.

***Implausible Professions: Arguments for Pluralism and Autonomy in Psychotherapy and Counselling*** – ed. Richard House and Nick Totton (PCCS Books, Ross-on-Wye, 1997) – a collection of work by many different authors from different modalities.

***Regulating the Psychological Therapies: From Taxonomy to Taxidermy*** – by Denis Postle (PCCS Books, 2007). Collected papers and articles critiquing state/statutory regulation and suggesting alternative possibilities.

***Psychoanalytic Practice and State Regulation*** – ed. Ian Parker and Simona Revelli (Karnac Books, London, 2008). A recent compilation of arguments.

The critiques in this book and the consultation proposals they point to continue a process of bringing into the open the culture that lies behind the HPC's administration and its public relations. A culture that seems as important as its catalogue of registrant injunctions. Lacanian psychoanalyst Janet Low maintains the HPCWatchDog blog in which she reports on visits to the HPC for meetings and hearings. See: http://hpcwatchdog.blogspot.com/

# A Tick-box Doxology?[1]

Denis Postle

*What the HPC commands it makes possible by its grace.*

The HPC Standards of proficiency for counselling and psychotherapy document has an aura, a resonance that has excited a lot of comment, not least from *e*lpnosis.[1] Scientised research validities, NHS-style managementspeak, 'threshold levels', a few afterthoughts specifically about counselling and psychotherapy, plus a culture of tick-box audit, all of it driven by coercion and the threat of punitive sanctions.

And yet in recognising and pillorying the icons of this technocratic culture, might we not have missed the bigger picture? I had a waking dream of the 'Standards' each being chanted, complete with its missing 'you must', over images of a circus in which animals did the bidding of the ringmaster with a whip.

And then it clicked; forget the circus, the cultural atmosphere the HPC Standards evoke is of centralised *ecclesiastical* power. Standards of proficiency for counselling and psychotherapy are a 'catechism' for compliance with a technocratic religion of belief and behaviour. And also for dealing with the non-compliance of heresy and heretics, *aka* charlatans.

The Standards are for ordinands and seminaries seeking entry to the new state church of Psychontology, in the diocese of New Labour False Promises. It seeks the conversion of the existing parishes, their present, past and future communicants. The latter through ensuring, through control of education and training, that any further development of psychontology will be according to the HPC articles of faith.

Let us not be in any doubt that this is a new religious departure, in many ways unlike previous churches. It reverses the dark resonant spaces with their music and incense into what it claims is complete transparency, in its meeting rooms Heavenly scrutiny is delivered via CCTV and hired in 'partners'. This is a church that has no bishops and that claims to have no theology, you can believe anything you like or nothing, but you must act according to the precepts set out in the Standards of proficiency catechism. Canon law details the sanctions for malfeasance up to and including excommunication.

Even a modest background in the sociology of institutions reveals the extent to which there is a theology, one that deifies scientised research and its RCTs and various related scientific heavens, of which the medical model of diagnosis and treatment and NHS-managerialism come most immediately to mind.

Is this just a silly mid-morning excursion driven by irritation at the gullibility of people thinking that if they sign up to the HPC's Standards of proficiency regime, regulatory grace will descend? I don't believe so. History is replete with churches, public and private, in which we create and sometimes try to enforce, definitions of human nature, what is human and natural. Humanity needed a Jesus, but courtesy of the Roman Empire's political agendas we got the Catholic Church. Henry VIII wanted a church that would do as it was told and so we have the Church of England, still with 26 bishops entitled to sit in the House of Lords.

As Jews know only too well, definitions of what counts as human and natural count. Become an Unmensch. Lose the right to life. When they are cementing over the meadows of psychological therapy diversity, collaborators in the dissolution of this previously rich ecology of mêtis and ethical values deny, or keep themselves alienated from, the historical evidence that in their need to define what is 'human and natural', religions almost without exception, create heresy, victimisation, exclusion and abuse. In a recent editorial, the dean of one of the UK sects, BACP chair Lynne Gabriel,[3] asked in effect (and affirmatively), would it not be part of the membership's task to denounce heretics?

I have written elsewhere about the HPC[4] having religious overtones, but the Standards of proficiency for counselling and psychotherapy bring this sharply into focus. Take a look at the beginning of that article and also, check out the father of all catechisms on the Vatican web-site[5] that has almost 3000 items. You could start with 2475: Offenses against Truth and then: 2850-54: Deliver us from Evil!

---

1 Doxology – a hymn of praise
2 http://ipnosis.postle.net
3 http://ipnosis.poslte.net/pages/BACPChairResponseJuly09.htm
4. http://ipnosis.postle.net/pages/HPCSpecial02.htm
5. http://www.vatican.va/archive/catechism/ccc_toc.htm

This article first appeared in August 2009 in *e*Ipnosis: http://ipnosis.postle.net

**IAN PARKER** is Professor of Psychology at Manchester Metropolitan University and a practising Lacanian psycho-analyst.

# Afterword
# THE STATE OF REGULATION TODAY
Ian Parker

This collection is a response to the attempt by the British government to regulate the activity of counsellors and psychotherapists through the Health Professions Council. This process is being marketed by the HPC as protection of the public, but really what it amounts to is protection of the rules that define what counselling and psychotherapy should look like. Bureaucratic micro-management of each aspect of the 'profession' is here designed to mesh counselling and psychotherapy into a slimmed-down NHS and to reduce treatment to short-term interventions that will get people off benefit and back to work. The questions that are addressed in the collection therefore resonate with a number of other pressing social issues.

This process of professionalisation and state regulation can be set in a broader context of the way expertise over mental health care is being managed now. Historically, women played a crucial part in care for others, including around what we now call 'mental health', and their own practice was excluded with the formation of professional medicine. Now, when many counsellors and psychotherapists are women – especially in the lower-status and more informal volunteer sectors – this professionalisation will side-line traditional stereotypically-feminine activity of care and social support. Health regulation will reduce therapy to procedures, techniques and targets to roll through as many people as quickly as possible, and so a crucial aspect of that work – time and space to speak and be taken seriously by another person – will be crushed out. You can guess already where women will figure, as the assistants in organisations and regulatory bodies run by men and, most important, running to an agenda that values stereotypically-masculine prediction and control of how we think and behave.

The attempt to regulate counselling and psychotherapy follows the regulation and 'protection' of titles of different kinds of psychologists in July this year, and the HPC realised that 'psychologist' is such a widespread term that it would be impossible to control who can and who cannot use it. Instead, different specific kinds of psychologist – clinical, educational and so on – will have their titles 'protected'. Now, as the HPC moves on to therapy regulation, the definitions are becoming more telling. A recent meeting of the 'Professional Liaison Group' set up by the HPC to bring together the great and good in the therapy world settled on definitions of therapy as 'treatment of the disordered mind' and counselling as concerned with 'mental health well-being'. The bureaucratic medical language used here to describe personal anguish says it all.

The segregation of different professionals into specific categories of expertise in the proposed regulation is also telling, and reinforces artificial distinctions that are not at work in other parts of the world. Here, humanistic and alternative and complementary counselling is at the bottom of the pecking order, with 'psychodynamic' approaches having just a little more status. Then psychotherapists have a little more power, especially if they are psychodynamic or 'psychoanalytic', and the top of the heap is mainstream psychoanalysis. You can guess what the difference is between how much it costs to train in each of these modalities, and how much you will pay if you go privately. It is no surprise, perhaps, that some have been hoping that their family and professional links with the medical profession and the House of Lords will make 'psychoanalysis' as such exempt from any regulation. At the very least, they would like psychoanalysis defined in such a way as to keep out the rabble. Now, with the HPC Professional Liaison Group controlled by psychoanalysts and those in awe of them, there is an attempt to divide and rule those who would like to be seen as health professionals, and status hierarchies will be fixed in place along the way if they succeed. They must not, and this collection is a clear voice of those who can see how wrong this attempt by the HPC to regulate our practice threatens to be.